New Daylig[ht]

Edited by Naomi Starkey   January–April 2014

New Daylight © BRF 2014

The Bible Reading Fellowship
15 The Chambers, Vineyard, Abingdon OX14 3FE
Tel: 01865 319700; Fax: 01865 319701
E-mail: enquiries@brf.org.uk; Website: www.brf.org.uk

ISBN 978 0 85746 030 1

Distributed in Australia by Mediacom Education Inc., PO Box 610, Unley, SA 5061.
Tel: 1800 811 311; Fax: 08 8297 8719;
E-mail: admin@mediacom.org.au
Available also from all good Christian bookshops in Australia.
For individual and group subscriptions in Australia:
Mrs Rosemary Morrall, PO Box W35, Wanniassa, ACT 2903.

Distributed in New Zealand by Scripture Union Wholesale, PO Box 760, Wellington
Tel: 04 385 0421; Fax: 04 384 3990; E-mail: suwholesale@clear.net.nz

Publications distributed to more than 60 countries

Acknowledgments
The New Revised Standard Version of the Bible, Anglicised Edition, copyright © 1989, 1995 by the
Division of Christian Education of the National Council of the Churches of Christ in the USA.
Used by permission. All rights reserved.

The Holy Bible, New International Version (Anglicised edition), copyright © 1979, 1984, 2011 by
Biblica. Used by permission of Hodder & Stoughton Publishers, an Hachette UK company. All
rights reserved. 'NIV' is a registered trademark of Biblica. UK trademark number 1448790.

The Holy Bible, Today's New International Version, copyright © 2004 by Biblica. Used by
permission of Hodder & Stoughton Publishers, an Hachette UK company. All rights reserved.
'TNIV' is a registered trademark of Biblica.

Extracts from the Authorised Version of the Bible (The King James Bible), the rights in which
are vested in the Crown, are reproduced by permission of the Crown's Patentee, Cambridge
University Press.

Extracts from The Book of Common Prayer of 1662, the rights of which are vested in the
Crown in perpetuity within the United Kingdom, are reproduced by permission of Cambridge
University Press, Her Majesty's Printers.

The Revised Common Lectionary is copyright © The Consultation on Common Texts, 1992 and is
reproduced with permission. *The Christian Year: Calendar, Lectionary and Collects*, which includes
the *Common Worship* lectionary (the Church of England's adaptations of the *Revised Common
Lectionary*, published as the Principal Service lectionary) is copyright © The Central Board of
Finance of the Church of England, 1995, 1997, and material from it is reproduced with
permission.

Printed by Gutenberg Press, Tarxien, Malta.

Suggestions for using *New Daylight*

Find a regular time and place, if possible, where you can read and pray undisturbed. Before you begin, take time to be still and perhaps use the BRF prayer. Then read the Bible passage slowly (try reading it aloud if you find it over-familiar), followed by the comment. You can also use *New Daylight* for group study and discussion, if you prefer.

The prayer or point for reflection can be a starting point for your own meditation and prayer. Many people like to keep a journal to record their thoughts about a Bible passage and items for prayer. In *New Daylight* we also note the Sundays and some special festivals from the Church calendar, to keep in step with the Christian year.

New Daylight and the Bible

New Daylight contributors use a range of Bible versions, and you will find a list of the versions used opposite, on page 2. You are welcome to use your own preferred version alongside the passage printed in the notes. This can be particularly helpful if the Bible text has been abridged.

New Daylight affirms that the whole of the Bible is God's revelation to us, and we should read, reflect on and learn from every part of both Old and New Testaments. Usually the printed comment presents a straight-forward 'thought for the day', but sometimes it may also raise questions rather than simply providing answers, as we wrestle with some of the more difficult passages of Scripture.

New Daylight is also available in a deluxe edition (larger format). Visit your local Christian bookshop or contact the BRF office, who can also give details about a cassette version for the visually impaired. For a Braille edition, contact St John's Guild, 8 St Raphael's Court, Avenue Road, St Albans, AL1 3EH.

Comment on *New Daylight*

To send feedback, you may email or write to BRF at the addresses shown opposite. If you would like your comment to be included on our website, please email connect@brf.org.uk. You can also Tweet to @brfonline, using the hashtag #brfconnect.

Writers in this issue

David Runcorn is a writer, spiritual director, theological teacher, retreat leader and conference speaker. He lives in Gloucester. You can meet him at www.davidruncorn.com.

Andrew John has been the Bishop of Bangor since 2008, having previously served all his ministry in the Diocese of St Davids. He is married to Caroline, who is also a deacon in the Church in Wales, and they have four children.

Naomi Starkey is a Commissioning Editor for BRF and edits and writes for *New Daylight* Bible reading notes. She has also written *The Recovery of Love* (BRF, 2012).

David Winter is retired from parish ministry. An honorary Canon of Christ Church, Oxford, he is well known as a writer and broadcaster. His most recent book for BRF is *At the End of the Day*.

Margaret Silf is an ecumenical Christian, committed to working across and beyond the denominational divides. She devotes herself to writing and accompanying others on their spiritual journey.

Michael Mitton is a freelance writer, speaker and consultant and the Fresh Expressions Adviser for the Derby Diocese. He is also the NSM Priest-in-charge of St Paul's Derby and honorary Canon of Derby Cathedral. He is the author of *Dreaming of Home* (BRF, 2012) and *Travellers of the Heart* (BRF, 2013).

Rachel Boulding is Deputy Editor of the *Church Times*. Before this, she was Senior Editor at SPCK Publishing, and then Senior Liturgy Editor at Church House Publishing. She lives in Dorset with her husband and son—and, during school terms, more than 70 teenage boys.

Tony Horsfall is a freelance trainer and retreat leader based in Yorkshire, with his own ministry, Charis Training. He is an elder of Ackworth Community Church and has written several books for BRF, including *Working from a Place of Rest* and *Servant Ministry*.

Lakshmi Jeffreys, as an Anglican priest, has served in parish ministry, university chaplaincy and as a mission officer across a diocese. She has recently undertaken church leadership in a village just outside Northampton.

Richard Fisher writes...

As the front cover shows, this issue marks the 25th anniversary of *New Daylight*. It's a milestone of special significance to me, as the launch of *New Daylight* in November 1988 was one of the first events that I was involved in, having joined BRF the previous month. The launch issue caused a real stir with its arresting cover image of a female coal miner!

The January–April 1989 issue of *New Daylight* brought a completely fresh, new approach. It replaced BRF's *Daylight* series, which, in 1979, had replaced the original Series B notes, first launched in 1929.

The vision for *New Daylight* came from its first editor, Shelagh Brown. Shelagh wanted to develop a relationship with the readers. In the past, the Bible readings had been written anonymously, but Shelagh drew together a team of regular contributors and included brief biographies so that readers could get a sense of who they were. Many have told us, over the years since, that they felt they knew those who wrote the notes.

Another innovation was that *New Daylight* was the first Bible reading notes series in the UK to include the printed Bible passage for each day. Some were concerned that this might discourage readers from looking up the passage in their own Bible. However, Shelagh's idea was to make it easy for people to take *New Daylight* with them, to read on the bus or train, at work, or on holiday; so it made sense for each issue to be self-contained. In addition, she pointed out that you couldn't assume any longer that everyone actually had a Bible of their own.

Over the last 25 years, *New Daylight* has only had three editors. Shelagh continued until her untimely death in June 1997. At that point, with absolutely no notice, David Winter, who had joined the writing team several years before, very kindly agreed to take on the role. He stepped down at the end of 2001, whereupon Naomi Starkey became editor alongside her role as commissioning editor for BRF books.

New Daylight continues to be BRF's flagship publication and one of the UK's bestselling Bible reading notes series. It continues to reflect the heart of BRF's vision: to connect people with God and resource their spiritual journey. As one reader recently put it, *New Daylight* brings us the treasures in the word of God each day.

Richard Fisher, Chief Executive

The BRF Prayer

Almighty God,
you have taught us that your word is a lamp for our feet
and a light for our path. Help us, and all who prayerfully
read your word, to deepen our fellowship with you
and with each other through your love.
And in so doing may we come to know you more fully,
love you more truly, and follow more faithfully
in the steps of your son Jesus Christ, who lives and reigns
with you and the Holy Spirit, one God for evermore.
Amen

The Beatitudes: 'How *happy* are you…!'

Over the next eleven days we will be reading and reflecting on the Beatitudes—those famous sayings that come at the beginning of the Sermon on the Mount in Matthew's Gospel.

In the ancient world, declaring someone 'blessed' was a way of congratulating them, for their place in life was clearly enviable and favoured. So the alternative English translation that begins these sayings with 'how *happy* are you…!' is correct. Although these blessings are enthusiastic in tone, who would envy anyone on this list? Those to whom Jesus says 'how *happy* are you!' are poor, hungry, powerless, mourning and persecuted. Yet, somehow, they are able to make peace with their circumstances.

Some might just stop reading at this point. Is this not an insensitive spiritualising of lives that have been hit hardest? There is another way of responding, however. We might allow the sheer strangeness of these sayings to jolt us into listening harder and more deeply to what Jesus is declaring here. Also, surely in a world like ours we would be wise not to pass up the offer of a blessed life too quickly.

What these sayings reveal are the signs of a world on the edge of transformation. These signs are all around us but easily hidden because they are where we least expect to look. If, however, life commonly experienced as God-forsaken is now being declared blessed, then something very new is going on. If God's blessing is found where it is normally assumed to be painfully absent, then there is hope. If the blessing of the transforming world of God's love is being poured out first in the darkest and loneliest corners of human experience, then no one and nowhere is beyond its reach.

These blessings come to us as both comfort and challenge. Comfort, because we are invited into a kingdom where our deepest human frailty and pain is 'blessed' and honoured. Challenge because these blessings are found among those following the way of Christ at its most costly.

These are the blessed signs of a kingdom that is coming—one that is beginning now, right here in our midst.

David Runcorn

His open eyes

When Jesus saw the crowds, he went up the mountain; and after he sat down, his disciples came to him. Then he began to speak, and taught them.

Notice where this all starts. We are told that 'Jesus saw the crowds' (v. 1). At the end of the previous chapter, we are told that 'great crowds followed him from Galilee, the Decapolis, Jerusalem, Judea, and from beyond the Jordan' (4:25). All that follows is because Jesus *notices*. What he sees is a crowded world of multiple, overwhelming troubles in need of healing and another way of living.

The sayings that follow are, interestingly, given to his disciples, not the crowd, which is a point that is commonly missed. There are many in the world whose quality of life reflects these sayings but would not claim to be Christian. Thank God they are there, but, here, Jesus is teaching his followers, and what he is describing ought to be the marks of the communities that are signs of his kingdom in the world.

Jesus' words here were a central inspiration to the prophetic German pastor Dietrich Bonhoeffer. Like Jesus, he looked out and he saw. What he saw was the tragic evil of a nation under Nazism, plunging headlong into the shadows of world war. He saw the need for a radically new vision of Christian community that could confront and resist evil and be a pointer to what life means in God's kingdom of love. A transformed church and world 'will surely come only from a life lived in accordance with the Sermon on the Mount', he wrote. 'I think it is time to gather people together to do this' (*Life Together*, 1939).

There is nothing sentimental about Jesus' sayings. Rather, they reveal radical and costly wisdom for shared life in a chaotic world. Like the first disciples, like Bonhoeffer and other faithful Christians through history, we need to come to Jesus and be taught the ways that will yet change this world.

Prayer
Lord, we see you still looking out on a world of such unending needs. Gather us to yourself and teach us how to be communities that offer another way of living.

DAVID RUNCORN

MATTHEW 5:3 (NRSV)

With open hands

'Blessed are the poor in spirit, for theirs is the kingdom of heaven.'

It is bitterly cold today. Just down the street, huddled up in his usual place under the arch, is a homeless man called Dave. While his situation shows that it is not good or blessed to be poor, it is not blessed to be rich either, according to Jesus. Luke's version adds a reverse of this saying and declares a fierce 'woe' on the wealthy, reminding them sternly that they have responsibilities to those who have not (Luke 6:24). Here, in Matthew, the blessing is pronounced on the poor 'in spirit', but we are not to imagine a blessed world of 'spirit' somewhere beyond this material world. Instead, 'spirit' here refers to our inmost response to *whatever* our worldly circumstances are, whether we are rich *or* poor, lifting this message above any 'us and them' arguments. After all, it is possible to be poor and totally mean or wealthy and wonderfully generous. Conversion of hearts and lives is as much a challenge to the worldly poor as it is to those burdened with many riches.

Poverty is actually a matter of ownership. The poor know only too well that (unless they resort to crime) much of what they need must come to them as gifts. The poor *in spirit* know that they own nothing in this world, for the earth is the Lord's, not ours (Psalm 24:1). Whatever fills our hands or pockets is held in trust and Luke's version reminds us that we are accountable for it. Every attempt to own and possess things for ourselves actually leaves others excluded and deprived. The root of all injustice is found here.

The poor in spirit are those who live life with open hands, giving as freely as they receive. As Paul wrote, they are 'poor, yet making many rich' (2 Corinthians 6:10). When we live in this spirit we not only reflect the life of heaven but also imitate the generosity of Jesus who, 'though he was rich... became poor'—a poverty that leaves us rich beyond imagining (8:9).

Prayer
Help me to live with open hands in the poverty of your kingdom.

DAVID RUNCORN

Grieving life

'Blessed are those who mourn, for they will be comforted.'

At first reading this can sound very insensitive. How can the shattering experience of grief and loss ever be blessed? If we read it from another perspective, though, there is a comforting promise here. It means exactly what it says—there is a blessing in the kingdom of God for negative emotion, for the tears, the anguish and the grief that go along with so much of our lives in this world. There is a blessing in the kingdom for the miserable! This does come as a relief when church is the hardest place to be because the mood is so upbeat and we feel we have to hide behind a smiling face rather than bring a dampener down on the faith of others. 'Weep with those who weep', wrote Paul (Romans 12:15). He did not say, 'Cheer them up'!

If there is a place in God where our griefs are welcome, honoured and even blessed, it means we can stop running from them—our own and those of others. While we are avoiding pain, there can be no real joy. Our capacity for rejoicing is in direct proportion to our capacity for sorrow.

This blessing is about something bigger than our own hurts, however. Blessed are those who are willing to stay discontented with the way things are—the injustice, oppression, uncertainty and unfairness of so much of life. A priest from a suffering African church once told me, 'Lament is what keeps the church in the Sudan alive!' We are called to be communities of blessed mourners who remain faithfully present to life's pain, who refuse easy answers, false comforts or distractions. We are not asked to do anything with it or 'make it better'—we must just be there. Some of the blessings in Jesus' sermon are in the future tense, but this promise is in the present, which tells us that whenever life must be mourned, God is with us.

Prayer

Lord, help me to honour the place of mourning—as you do—in my own life and in the lives of those around me.

DAVID RUNCORN

MATTHEW 5:5 (NRSV)

Trust and promise

'Blessed are the meek, for they will inherit the earth.'

To be completely honest, it is not easy to feel excited about a world inherited by the 'meek'! The English word is commonly used to describe people who are rather weak, diffident, ineffectual and mouse-like, but this translation is most unhelpful. After all, the first hearers of this blessing knew that Moses, who overthrew the might of the Egyptian armies, was *commended* for his meekness (Numbers 12:3, KJV: the Hebrew word can also be translated as 'poor'). This passage is, in fact, a quotation from Psalm 37 (v. 11), which gives us the context we need to understand what Jesus' teaching is here. The word 'meek' is used in the psalm to refer to the underdogs, the disinherited and the voiceless of this world—those totally outside the places of power and without any influence on them. The psalmist urges them not to get worked up about those who 'have it all'. Do not envy them, he advises, for anybody living as if what they achieve and gain is their own is living in an unreal world. It cannot last because it is not true, so we should not fall into the same trap by seeking what they seek.

Perhaps, in an almost mischievous way, this blessing is saying to the deprived and meek, 'turn this to your advantage'. Those without power or possessions cannot be powerful and possessive, so blessed are those unable to achieve such things. Why? Because power is not for owning or achieving in your own right, it is God's. Listen, though, to the second half of the blessing—the meek will actually inherit 'the earth'. An inheritance is not earned or achieved, nor is it an obligation, but a pure gift. That is what God is like. The meek are those who live in utter, trusting dependence on God for everything. Against all the odds and outward appearances, they will inherit it all.

Prayer

Lord, I pray for meekness to receive this blessing. 'Be still before the Lord, and wait patiently for him; do not fret over those who prosper… it only leads to evil' (Psalm 37:7–8).

DAVID RUNCORN

11

Waiting without

> 'Blessed are those who hunger and thirst for righteousness, for they will be filled.'

In the creation story at the beginning of the Bible, sin enters the world as the result of disordered appetites. Adam and Eve take what is not theirs to take; they covet and consume what is simply not good for them. What we call the Fall is the tragic indulging in misguided desire. So, we should not be surprised to hear, as we do here, that the way to a world remade and blessed as God always intended must begin with the willingness to stay hungry and thirsty for what most truly nourishes us in life.

This 'going without' is not a punishment; being hungry and thirsty is hard, but it is not wrong. The problem is that our appetites and desires do not do what they are meant to do: they lead us *away* from what is deeply satisfying and filling. We persist in pursuing unhealthy diets, which may fill us but leave us dulled and sleepy, not more alive. It is not surprising that eating disorders are such a feature of our consumer world. Today's blessing comes when our appetites are redirected towards what alone can assuage our hunger.

The question behind these words is, 'Are you willing to wait?' The blessed hungry and thirsty are those who are prepared to stay empty and dissatisfied for the sake of a better world. Being hungry for 'righteousness' takes this blessing beyond our own lives and personal needs. This is nothing less than a longing for justice in a world where so many go without and life and its resources are not shared fairly. Jesus' words call us to have no appetite for any kind of life which is not life that can be shared and enjoyed by all. We are called to be hungry for justice. In the wild, the hungry go hunting and so must we—we must go out and stalk a better world. Jesus promises that such a hunger will be blessed and satisfied.

Prayer
Lord, may my appetite for life involve an appetite for a world where no one goes without.

DAVID RUNCORN

Unjudging love

'Blessed are the merciful, for they will receive mercy.'

In the kingdom of God a simple—but non-negotiable—law of cause and effect operates. What you give is what you receive. You want to receive? Then you must first give. You want to be forgiven? Then you must forgive. You seek mercy? Then be merciful. The initiative lies with us. This can take courage, especially if we have been hurt or betrayed in life. It is so tempting to hold back, saying (with apparent politeness), 'You first'. There is no risk-free living on offer here, though. If we try to keep the door that leads us out to others 'safely' barred, we also close their way in to us. We cannot have it both ways. We need to hear this blessing and we need to practise trusting it.

Now, why does mercy receive a special blessing here? Precisely because we spend so much time doing exactly the opposite. Religion is all too easily experienced as a way of judging and condemning, not as mercy. History shows that the more fervent and devoted a faith becomes, the more prone it is to becoming hard, cruel and excluding. This is nowhere more starkly illustrated than in the cross of Jesus. It has been wisely said that human beings 'never do evil so completely and cheerfully as when they do it from religious conviction' (Pascal, 1623–62).

The merciful are those who know their share in the wrongness of things. They offer no resistance to this truth: resistance is what happens when we are judging others. When we judge, we stand apart from those we condemn, but this isolates us, too. No wonder we become hardened. The merciful, instead, stand *alongside* others. They are those who know exactly what life is like and know that change must begin with themselves. Practising mercy is not for faint hearts. What frees us to be generous in giving mercy is the knowledge that we can leave the judging to God.

Reflection

Can you think of people or individuals you tend to judge? What might it mean to show them mercy? Pray for them to be blessed.

DAVID RUNCORN

With clear vision

'Blessed are the pure in heart, for they will see God.'

The orange juice I drank at breakfast claimed to be 'pure', meaning that it had no artificial additives in it—it was nothing but natural juice. When something is pure, it is what it says it is. 'Pure' drinking water is safe to drink because there are no harmful bacteria in it. When something is pure, we can trust its goodness. What about a pure heart? We might expect Jesus' teaching to stress the pollution of evil and sin, but he chooses to stress something else instead. This blessing links purity with clear vision and the ability to see God.

In the Bible, the heart is not the centre of feelings; it is the innermost centre of who I truly am—body, mind and spirit; it is the 'real me'. To be pure in heart, then, is to come from a place of truth, health and clear vision.

The problem is that our hearts are such busy, cluttered places. They are full of restless plans and confused intentions about who we are and what we want. Religious clutter is as distracting as any, perhaps more so. This means that our hearts are like muddy ponds; everything is so constantly stirred up that nothing ever settles, the water is never pure and clear. As a result, we see nothing with any depth or clarity, whether good or bad.

To begin to be pure in heart we must simply learn to be still, not trying to be or do or feel anything. We just need to be still and quiet in God's presence. Our settling only comes from a deepening capacity to receive God's accepting love—the one who sees us as we are and loves us still. Slowly, as our hearts settle in that truth, our lives gain new clarity and we will see more clearly. In fact, the pure in heart see *everything* clearly, as it truly is, uncontaminated and undistorted by anything that is false. And, as nothing is outside God's sustaining love, we shall start to encounter God everywhere.

Prayer
Lord, help my heart to settle so that I may see you in all things.

DAVID RUNCORN

In the breach

'Blessed are the peacemakers, for they will be called children of God.'

'We pray for peace in the world.' Is any prayer said with more frequency and longing in a world like ours? How easily these words can feel empty and powerless in terms of changing anything much!

Well, this blessing assumes that we are part of the answer to that prayer. Peacemaking is prayer in action. This means turning away from a helpless dependency that waits in hope that someone else will solve it. We *can* make a difference, but it is costly, for there can be no peacemaking without facing and meeting what keeps us apart from each other.

Peacemakers make their home in the midst of all that is separated, and this is where the church is called to live out its life. We are not alone, though, because this is where Jesus is. The first Christians often imagined the death of Christ as like breaking down a dividing wall of hostility (Ephesians 2:14). This world, forever more, has been breached. A break has been made in the deadly cycles of violence in this world and, in that breach, new meetings are possible. Relationships can begin to change; trust can replace suspicion. Through the breach the life of a new kingdom flows, bringing healing and renewing hope. Some experience this breach of grace as a sudden freedom to respond in love where before there was hatred. More often, it is like a regular bathing, cleansing and rebinding of deep wounds that will not quickly heal and remain vulnerable to reinfection.

At the end of Christian worship, we are often sent out with the words 'Go in peace.' This is not about feeling 'peaceful', we are being invited to enter somewhere. Think of it as 'go *into* peace'. Go into the place where the love of Christ is making new community possible. Go into the breach that is the cross of Christ, where his arms stretch out across all that divides and brings everything together in his own body. Peacemakers are children of God because they bear his likeness and act in his ways.

Prayer
Lord, help me to be a person who leads others into your peace.

DAVID RUNCORN

15

Up against it

'Blessed are those who are persecuted for righteousness' sake, for theirs is the kingdom of heaven.'

Immediately after the peacemakers are blessed, there comes a blessing on those persecuted for the sake of the gospel. There is good reason for this, because this is the price of peacemaking. It is a tragically familiar feature of conflict everywhere that it is not the extremists on either side who are singled out, but those in the middle, the bridge-builders. These are the ones who could make the difference, bring together warring sides and so effect a change. They are intercessors—a word that means 'stand between'. As we saw yesterday, the cross is an image of this: it is planted in the middle, reaching out on either side and so offering a place of meeting.

Near where I live is a monument marking the spot where, in a more intolerant and violent age, a Christian leader was burned at the stake for his faith. It reminds me that people pay with their lives for the faith I own. They still do. In the last hundred years, more people have died for their faith around the world than in the rest of Christian history put together. As I pass that memorial each morning, I pray for people in the world today who, at whatever cost to themselves, will speak words of truth, peace and reconciliation; whose example and actions may confront and challenge; whose presence may inspire a change of heart or avert violence. I pray for those who today will face rejection, violence and even death for what they stand for. I bless them for their life and example and pray that, in whatever way is mine to do, I will be the same presence for the sake of the one I follow.

We are called to intercede. This is where Christians make their home on earth—with Christ in the face of hostility and rejection. It will cost us, too, but we will be blessed.

Prayer
We pray for those who today will be persecuted for their faith.
We ask for courage to follow their example and willingness to be known for what we believe.

David Runcorn

Insulted lives

'Blessed are you when people revile you and persecute you and utter all kinds of evil against you falsely on my account. Rejoice and be glad, for your reward will be great in heaven, for in the same way they persecuted the prophets who were before you.'

These verses are an extension of yesterday's blessing, but here the focus shifts. Until now the blessings have been pronounced in general terms for 'they'—those out there who are living the life of the kingdom. Now, it is as if Jesus turns and faces us personally: 'Blessed are *you*'. These are no longer general principles for anyone listening: 'I am talking to *you*, here and now.' If Jesus is speaking personally, he is near us in person—and never more so than when life is costly on his account.

He urges us to respond with the wildest possible enthusiasm whenever we suffer because we follow him (and notice, there is no question that we will suffer). To Matthew's 'rejoice and 'be (exceedingly) glad', Luke adds 'and leap for joy' (Luke 6:23). Why? Not because suffering is good. The challenge of this response is that it lifts our eyes beyond a preoccupation with ourselves. It helps us realise that this is part of a much bigger and more glorious story that is yet to be revealed but can strengthen and encourage us now. This was even so for Jesus. We read that it was for the 'joy that was set before him' that he endured the cross (Hebrews 12:2). Richard Wurmbrand, a Romanian pastor who suffered years of torture and solitary confinement in a communist jail, used to dance in his cell every night in obedience to these words, leaving his jailers bewildered by what they were seeing.

In our suffering, however slight it is in comparison to that of the saints, we are standing in a glorious flow of history, with all who have gone before us and suffered for a vision worth anything and everything to be part of. Rejoice: we are in amazing company.

Prayer
Lord, when faith is costly, help me to rejoice and find myself in the bigger story and in the company of the saints.

David Runcorn

Soaking in—standing out

'You are the salt of the earth; but if salt has lost its taste, how can its saltiness be restored? It is no longer good for anything, but is thrown out and trampled underfoot. You are the light of the world. A city built on a hill cannot be hidden. No one after lighting a lamp puts it under the bushel basket, but on the lampstand, and it gives light to all in the house. In the same way, let your light shine before others, so that they may see your good works and give glory to your Father in heaven.'

'Pass the salt' is one of the basic phrases of table manners in most parts of the world. Salt is an essential part of a healthy diet. It also adds flavour to what we eat. In hot climates, before refrigeration was invented, it was vital for preserving food. It was also used as a disinfectant: Luke mentions that salt was used on the dung heap (Luke 14:35). Similarly, the presence of Christians in the world is health-giving and stimulates the flavour and celebration of life. It is also a vital preservative, resisting corruption and decay. To be that kind of presence, we must be *close* to the world. There is no living at a safe, 'pure' distance. Rather, by the grace of God, our presence absorbs and seals off what would otherwise cause corruption.

It is very possible that when Jesus referred to a 'city on a hill', he was looking up to the hills around Galilee where even a relatively small group of houses would stand out clearly against the skyline—nothing could be hidden. It was a perfect visual aid for his message. The presence of Christians in the world should also be visible and make other things visible, just as light does. This light of Christian presence reveals in two ways. It overcomes the darkness of life for everyone, offering a way to see clearly. Even more importantly, it casts light on the character of God, revealing him as the loving Father and the life of heaven.

Prayer
Lord, give me the courage to stand close but also to stand out in this world.

DAVID RUNCORN

The big issue

In John's Gospel we read these words from Jesus: 'A new command I give you: love one another. As I have loved you, so you must love one another. By this everyone will know that you are my disciples, if you love one another' (John 13:34–35). This command has one very clear goal, which is that everyone will know the disciples belong to Jesus. We read elsewhere similar statements about the requirement to go beyond words (for example, Matthew 7:16).

This series, which I have called 'The big issue', is all about the way Christians—and churches—should love each other. It is intended to explore, therefore, Jesus' command. We will examine the things that promote love and trust and the challenges, too. We will not confine ourselves to the New Testament, but, rather, see how, throughout the Bible, the togetherness of God's people has always been God's wish. This biblical ecumenism is not a matter of agreeing at any cost and is certainly not intended to provide a cloak to avoid hard and searching questions about truth and error. Sometimes unity has been misunderstood and the terrible consequences of poor accountability have led to many being damaged. Rightly understood, the message is that our witness to the saving love of Christ is tightly bound up with our being one body. This great vision remains today and must be heard afresh if we are to respond to the world around us faithfully. I pray it will inspire and provoke us, leading to a new search for the uniting love that blesses and glorifies God.

'I pray also for those who will believe in me through their message, that all of them may be one, Father, just as you are in me and I am in you. May they also be in us so that the world may believe that you have sent me' (John 17:20–21).

God of unity and truth, call us to love one another in new ways. Give us fresh vision and desire to move towards each other in bold faith. Keep the doubts at bay and may fear be overcome by that perfect love shown and offered to us by your Son, Jesus Christ. Amen

Andrew John

Let God be God

Brothers and sisters, I could not address you as spiritual but as worldly—mere infants in Christ. I gave you milk, not solid food, for you were not yet ready for it. Indeed, you are still not ready. You are still worldly. For since there is jealousy and quarrelling among you, are you not worldly? Are you not acting like mere human beings? For when one says, 'I follow Paul,' and another, 'I follow Apollos,' are you not mere human beings? What, after all, is Apollos? And what is Paul? Only servants, through whom you came to believe—as the Lord has assigned to each his task. I planted the seed, Apollos watered it, but God has been making it grow.

Some readers will recall the hilarious exchange between Eric Morecambe and André Previn. The wonderful riposte was Eric's: 'I'm playing all the right notes but not necessarily in the right order'! There is sometimes a tendency in the church to lose sight of the first-order issues and their impact on other matters.

Here, Paul sets out the right agenda for the Corinthian Christians and the right order, too. The truth is, the Corinthian Christians were riven by jealousies and divisions that threatened to ruin their life together. Power struggles and other attempts to assert competing allegiances over and against other believers were having a disastrous effect. Paul firmly places God at the heart of the issue (v. 6) and so establishes the foundation for all relationships between believers and churches.

If God remains at the centre of our lives, our worship and our planning, we are better placed to build God-honouring communities. Paul does not leave the matter there: those who belong to God can see themselves as servants (v. 5), whose motivation is not self-advancement but the good of the church. This might mean that we are less visible and do not always 'win' the arguments, but it can lead to something much better and more worthwhile, something much more Christlike.

Prayer

Lord Jesus, may your greatness become ever more important to me so that I see others as you do and myself as your servant and that service as life itself. Amen

ANDREW JOHN

The point of delivery

Just as a body, though one, has many parts, but all its many parts form one body, so it is with Christ. For we were all baptised by one Spirit so as to form one body—whether Jews or Gentiles, slave or free—and we were all given the one Spirit to drink.

There are few images more powerful than the one that Paul uses in today's passage. He describes the company of Christians as the body of Christ.

In order to be absolutely clear with the Corinthians as to the essential nature of their new identity, he presents a picture of how they belong to each other in a special way. For Paul, it was vital that his friends understood it was God who was responsible for this. Christians are drawn into fellowship, whoever they are, by the Spirit (v. 13). The church can therefore never be thought of as a club or association with loose connections between members or attendees. The many parts of this 'body' form something living and whole, just as a human body is living and whole.

It is easy to see where Paul wants to take this image. A body has an identity; it can respond to events around it. A body can grow (or shrink!), feel joy and pain; it can create and destroy. The one thing it cannot do, though, is function as a body if the members are apart.

So, there is a clear challenge at the heart of this analogy: a church that is divided or where parts of it are held apart or choosing to split apart falls far short of the apostle's exhortation. We will examine the wider implications for churches together a little later as we look at the passages over the following days, but we can be clear about two things: God is the author of this new creation that is the church, the body of Christ, and there is an implied mandate requiring Christians to remain as one body.

Prayer

God of truth and purpose, give your people a strong sense of your call to live as one body and to work for a common life that reflects your identity as one God, yet Father, Son and Holy Spirit. Amen

ANDREW JOHN

A neat trick?

All the believers were one in heart and mind. No one claimed that any of their possessions was their own, but they shared everything they had. With great power the apostles continued to testify to the resurrection of the Lord Jesus. And God's grace was so powerfully at work in them all that there was no needy person among them. For from time to time those who owned land or houses sold them, brought the money from the sales and put it at the apostles' feet, and it was distributed to anyone who had need.

In Acts, we not only see the life of the first Christians but are also given a vision of what the church can be, a kind of template for living the gospel. Today's passage offers a challenging example of the high quality of service that was offered to both God and the church. Look at the language used: '*All* the believers… they shared *everything* they had' (v. 32). These are big words.

We are told that a clear confidence in the resurrection fuelled this outpouring of service (v. 33): because the church knew the power of the resurrection, it could be dynamic in its outer life of service. The resurrection makes it possible to overcome human selfishness. If the cross speaks of God's forgiveness, the resurrection speaks of new life.

The consequence of this dynamic faith being expressed in dynamic action was a unity that the church has seldom, if ever, (re)possessed. I think that tells us something about the way togetherness is generated. It is not a togetherness without any room for difference or disagreement, or the kind in which Christians are unable to challenge and be challenged, which is sometimes how unity is described and understood. Instead, it is a togetherness that is stronger than the human tendency to assert, misuse power and insist that one person's or group's agenda prevails over those of others. There is a strength when Christians are united that is not about power so much as loving service. Churches that model this way of living have the capacity to transform many lives.

Prayer

God of truth and love, give us a sense of what it means to live dynamic lives of faith in Jesus and service to others. And let it begin in me. Amen

ANDREW JOHN

The big picture

I pray that out of his glorious riches he may strengthen you with power through his Spirit in your inner being, so that Christ may dwell in your hearts through faith. And I pray that you, being rooted and established in love, may have power, together with all the Lord's people, to grasp how wide and long and high and deep is the love of Christ, and to know this love that surpasses knowledge—that you may be filled to the measure of all the fullness of God.

Psychologists tell us that personality is hugely influential in how we see the world. Some people tend to see the nuts and bolts, while others see the big picture and make less sense of its composite parts. There is no right or wrong about this, but it does help us understand how we differ from one another.

In today's passage, we are given a big picture that is one of the greatest in the New Testament. It is intended to inspire and encourage us—and it contains a prayer that Christians should understand and know God as God really is. That is the platform on which discipleship and loving service are built.

The author's focus encompasses everyone—the whole church: 'together with *all* the Lord's people' (v. 18). What lies at the very heart of our existence as Christians is the love of God, which we are called to know and experience more completely each day. I am quite certain that it is impossible for churches to love each other and work together without the love of Christ. To put it another way, the degree to which we cannot love each other or recognise Christ in one another is the degree to which the love of Christ is either present, or absent, in us all. How would you describe your church today?

Prayer

Heavenly Father, I pray that out of your glorious riches you will strengthen us so that Jesus may dwell in our hearts by faith. May we be rooted in love and grasp the width, length, height and depth of his love and see one another in the light of this. Amen

ANDREW JOHN

What? God's not an Anglican?!

Now when Joshua was near Jericho, he looked up and saw a man standing in front of him with a drawn sword in his hand. Joshua went up to him and asked, 'Are you for us or for our enemies?' 'Neither,' he replied, 'but as commander of the army of the Lord I have now come.' Then Joshua fell face down to the ground in reverence, and asked him, 'What message does my Lord have for his servant?' The commander of the Lord's army replied, 'Take off your sandals, for the place where you are standing is holy.' And Joshua did so.

The Old Testament is replete with stories of the unexpected. Just as you think you have a handle on what God will do next, God does something quite different. Take Joshua, the man appointed by God to complete the task entrusted to Moses, who turned the Hebrews back to faithful observation of the Law regarding circumcision and celebrated the Passover in the desert. We might think that he had the ear of the Almighty. Then the unexpected answer comes: '"Neither," he replied, "but as commander of the army of the Lord I have now come"' (v. 14). For Joshua, the answer required a change of outlook. God was not on his 'side'; God was not a power to be wielded for personal gain, and not some kind of trophy with which to threaten or cajole others.

For many Christians, the most significant thing about the church is the character and quality of life experienced within it. Even as convictions about sacraments, government and forms of service are maintained, still the most important matter remains the essential life of the body, its mission and ministry. We discover Christ in many churches and experience the Spirit of God in many places. It is at this point that we must recognise God is a great deal bigger and better than our denominations. Quite literally, God is not on our side. Wisdom, however, asks a better kind of question: 'Will we be on God's side?'

Prayer

God of truth, you show no partiality. Teach us the way of humble love and give us new eyes to see you wherever you may be found. In Christ's name. Amen.

Andrew John

Reframing the question

Jesus, knowing their thoughts, took a little child and made him stand beside him. Then he said to them, 'Whoever welcomes this little child in my name welcomes me; and whoever welcomes me welcomes the one who sent me. For whoever is least among you all is the greatest.' 'Master,' said John, 'we saw someone driving out demons in your name and we tried to stop him, because he is not one of us.' 'Do not stop him,' Jesus said, 'for whoever is not against you is for you.'

Ordained ministers are responsible for many services, not least of which are funerals. The number of times I have been told that the deceased requested the song 'I did it my way' is bewildering. To me this is the epitome of what is wrong with human beings—we always want to 'do it our way'!

In today's passage, Jesus commends attitudes that are quite the opposite—one of which should characterise our relationships with each other and one with those beyond our immediate circle. The first is humility: whoever welcomes children shows the way of the kingdom, as such lowliness has become—in the words of the hymn—'inner clothing' that fits us well. It avoids the tendency to place the concerns and interests of others beneath our own.

It is this that lies at the heart of many divisions between Christians. Such divisions are often cloaked in theological and scriptural language but are really an excuse for our personal ambitions. I am grateful to a friend for sharing the idea of LG—a 'loose grip'. This reflects what Jesus commended in the one ministering outside the company of the apostles (vv. 49–50). A 'loose grip' recognises signs of God at work beyond us and rejoices in it rather than seeking to control it. Where such attitudes flourish, there is no room for destructive divisions.

Prayer

Holy God, send your Spirit so that holy and healthy attitudes inhabit the life of your church. Forgive what we have been, help us to amend what we are and set a course for us in the future where our communal life reveals your glory. Amen

ANDREW JOHN

Doing the stuff

A crowd was sitting around [Jesus], and they told him, 'Your mother and brothers are outside looking for you.' 'Who are my mother and my brothers?' he asked. Then he looked at those seated in a circle round him and said, 'Here are my mother and my brothers! Whoever does God's will is my brother and sister and mother.'

The Gospels include various repeated themes, surely indicating that they have a special importance in the kingdom of God. Today's passage is on one such theme—Jesus describing his family as those who do God's will (vv. 34–35). With a dramatic gesture, he asserts that his family is not founded in flesh and blood at all, but in action and obedience.

I recently began to teach my son to drive our car. We both survived the experience, but what struck me afresh in the process is how some things require practice and dedication. Solid lessons are thus learned that cannot simply be instantly downloaded into the inbox of life experiences; they have to be acquired by working at them. As I reflect on the life of the church in general, I feel that leaders (myself included) bear a responsibility for some of the issues that continue to separate us. We do not practise the shared life we profess to love. A journey that involves 'outsiders' can be threatening and appear less of an adventure and more of a trial. So we opt for safety and do less than we could—much less than we should.

Churches that are open to God have a character that is attractive and healthy. They are prepared to shift and be changed by what they encounter. This confidence is wise and mature, well-rooted and secure, yet still vulnerable. As we think about Jesus' call to be 'doers', we might ask ourselves what 'doing' is required of us in relation to brothers and sisters in other churches—especially ones that are quite different and, we might think, not part of the 'family'.

Prayer

Lord Jesus Christ, make me a doer whose actions forge strong and holy relationships. Give me new grace to venture in faith so that you are found in the journey and glorified in our weaknesses. Amen

ANDREW JOHN

Warning: fragile goods

Make every effort to keep the unity of the Spirit through the bond of peace.

Soundbites are often given a bad press, said to be lacking finesse or simply inadequate. While such criticism is sometimes fair, a strapline or key message can be powerful, too. How many advertisements do we remember simply because of a single memorable phrase? Today, we have a single line of text to ponder. I hope it, too, will be memorable.

What does it mean to keep the unity of the Spirit through the bond of peace? Here are some practical ways in which churches can respond to this verse. First, churches that consciously share worship on a regular basis create a bond of peace. I thank God for a Methodist colleague who, when the Methodist building fell down, saw the potential to build relationships with other churches, as well as a new place of worship of their own. Christmas and Easter celebrations were shared and numerous monthly gatherings fostered joint outreach and mission.

Second, working together creates a bond of peace. If churches share planning and activity, not only does it prevent a return to old separatist attitudes but it also draws new energy into a broader environment. Amen We are able to be more effective if greater resources are released in mission together. We can share children's work, youth ventures, social transformation projects—the list could go on.

Lastly, an attitude of wondering creates a bond of peace. This means talking and listening together—to God as well as one another. We need to hear the stories of times past that have formed us into who we are in the present. We need to look to see the points of convergence and difference. We need to ask new questions about where God's future might be for us all, and allow these thoughts to bubble and change as we wonder and ponder. Such a holy and open endeavour is rich with potential.

Prayer

Create in your church the unity of the Spirit, O God, in a bond of peace. Open our hearts to the wisdom of risk and journeying and may good things come from lives venturing together. For Jesus Christ's sake. Amen

ANDREW JOHN

1 Kings 12:6–7 (TNIV)

Disaster

Then King Rehoboam consulted the elders who had served his father Solomon during his lifetime. 'How would you advise me to answer these people?' he asked. They replied, 'If today you will be a servant to these people and serve them and give them a favourable answer, they will always be your servants.'

If yesterday's passage showed how to build a positive unity, today's is all about avoiding catastrophe (see vv. 1–17 for the full story). A new king receives a delegation with a complaint about leadership style and seeks advice from two different groups. The outcome is a harsh and uncompromising rejection of the demands for mercy. The result is unsurprising: disaster.

The responsibility of exercising power is a heavy one, and the challenge is to exercise it justly and effectively. In the Gospels, we see a new expression of power characterised by service (Matthew 20:26). Jesus gave his blessing and permission to the disciples to preach and heal (Mark 6:8–13), but this was not an act of delegation so much as a sharing in the work of the kingdom, and he was quick to offer encouragement and correction (Luke 10:20). By contrast, King Rehoboam understood power as an act of coercion. He tried to prevail over those complaining and subdue them by means of his office and authority. This approach failed spectacularly. There are important lessons here for Christians, especially in the way we relate to others and other churches. Self-serving power is not only idolatrous and doomed to fail but is the very opposite of what Jesus commended and commanded. Ultimately it destroys trust, deprives the coerced of responsibility and those who wield the power of the God-given vulnerability that all leaders need.

We should pray for a searching and deeply mature wisdom that allows our motives to be tested and questioned. With such wisdom there is the hope of godly leadership.

Prayer

Serving and loving God, give me a heart and mind that know themselves in both weakness and hope. May my ambitions become ever your own and my actions bring blessing and liberty, for the sake of Christ. Amen

ANDREW JOHN

Fighting the dogs of war

Finally, brothers and sisters, whatever is true, whatever is noble, whatever is right, whatever is pure, whatever is lovely, whatever is admirable—if anything is excellent or praiseworthy—think about such things. Whatever you have learned or received or heard from me, or seen in me—put it into practice. And the God of peace will be with you.

Even though I do not have a medical background, I love the idea of an antidote—something that counters a poison, diminishes its effectiveness and protects vital functions. As Paul begins to conclude his letter to the Philippians, he commends a wide range of Christian disciplines, all of which have antidote-like properties.

In this series of passages we have been focusing on connecting the message of our Bible readings to both individual disciples and churches together. Although today's passage is not confined to individuals, it actually makes most sense when related to them. Paul's concern is not the avoidance of conflict, nor is it an invitation to a weak, paper-thin Christianity, which uses niceties to cover up serious matters. What he is calling for is something grounded and resolute in spirit. First, he commends attitudes that are distinctly Christlike (v. 8). This implies a robust spirituality that is unlikely to be found where spiritual discipline is lacking; it requires effort. Second, he commends the sustained practice of such attitudes (v. 9). When I go to the gym following a period of absence, I know I will struggle with a regime that I normally find manageable, because I am out of practice. Paul's words here have the idea of continuity built into them: we cannot afford any 'periods of absence'.

The implications for unity are obvious. Keeping a grip on any attitudes that lead to division and discord is vital for the health of any Christian and any church. However we might dress up division, it is almost always rooted in poor spiritual relationships—with God and with others. This is an area where practice makes perfect.

Prayer

Lord Jesus, give me strength to work at those disciplines that are difficult and wisdom to see the effort as being worthwhile. For your sake. Amen

ANDREW JOHN

Down to earth

'If you will not [accept a gift from me],' said Naaman, 'please let me, your servant, be given as much earth as a pair of mules can carry, for your servant will never again make burnt offerings and sacrifices to any other god but the Lord. But may the Lord forgive your servant for this one thing... when I bow down in the temple of Rimmon, may the Lord forgive your servant for this.'

Naaman has been healed of leprosy (vv. 1–14) and now asks Elisha if he can take some earth home with him—a piece of the land of Israel. This might sound absurd to us, but faith at that time was strongly attached to the land. The 'gods' were believed to be territorial, so, by taking earth from Israel, Naaman's intention was to take the God of Israel with him. Second, there is the matter of Rimmon, the god whom Naaman serves. His task was to support his master as he entered the temple and show due reverence for their god. Naaman, sensing there is something desperately lacking in this, asks for Elisha's forbearance and understanding.

The request for earth shows the power of territory to shape convictions and understanding. My experience is that this is also true of the church. We easily end up believing that God can only work in this place or that, in this ministry or that. We limit God and shut our minds to those who find God elsewhere and in different ways. In his question about the temple of Rimmon, however, we see the possibility of change. Naaman is on a journey, not just back to his land but also towards the God whose power and worth he has experienced. If his first request shows misunderstanding, the second offers the hope of God's grace bringing true understanding. If we allow our attitudes to be shaped by such hope, great potential can be released for the lives of our churches today.

Prayer

God of surprises, may we discover new joy as we find you in unexpected ways. Give us eyes to see beyond our own experience and grace to respond with open faith. For Christ's sake. Amen

ANDREW JOHN

Now what do you see?

'My servant David will be king over them, and they will all have one shepherd. They will follow my laws and be careful to keep my decrees. They will live in the land I gave to my servant Jacob, the land where your ancestors lived. They and their children and their children's children will live there forever... I will make a covenant of peace with them... and I will put my sanctuary among them for ever. My dwelling-place will be with them; I will be their God, and they will be my people.'

At this point I want to ask a provocative question: what is the value of unity anyway? Very often it sits near the bottom of a church's agenda. Whatever words we use in public, our actions may tell a different story about our real priorities.

Ezekiel's vision in the latter part of chapter 37 (less well-known than the valley of dry bones), speaks of God bringing the separated together for two important reasons. The first is the restoration of a good and holy relationship with God. The prophet speaks of a new king and shepherd (v. 24) to lead and guide, a new inheritance and covenant to nourish and nurture (vv. 25–26) and a new dwelling-place for God with his people (v. 27). We must not lose this strong sense that unity and a relationship with God belong together.

Second, this hope is fulfilled in Jesus, but the oneness of God's chosen people is a part of this fulfilment. Such a vision should inspire the church at a fundamental level. It can help us to shape a common life rather than swiftly moving to the things that divide us. What is known as the Lund Principle (after the location of the 1952 World Council of Churches conference) comes to mind: that is, we should act together in all matters except those in which deep differences of conviction compel us to act separately. What would the church look like if it modelled itself on this principle? What would we change and what new things would we do?

Prayer

Living Lord, help your church to see a big picture and yearn for a unity we currently lack. For Christ's sake. Amen

ANDREW JOHN

Made for this

So from now on we regard no one from a worldly point of view. Though we once regarded Christ in this way, we do so no longer. Therefore, if anyone is in Christ, the new creation has come: the old has gone, the new is here! All this is from God, who reconciled us to himself through Christ and gave us the ministry of reconciliation, that God was reconciling the world to himself in Christ, not counting people's sins against them. And he has committed to us the message of reconciliation. We are therefore Christ's ambassadors, as though God were making his appeal through us.

Any web search of the phrase 'In God's country' will produce an endless assortment of ideas, films, pictures and songs. Most of them are rather fanciful, though there is a uniting theme that something different, good and worthy is to be found in such a place (wherever it might actually be!). Paul, however, writing to the Corinthian Christians in today's passage, takes the same idea down a very different track, suggesting that where God abides, there is reconciliation. For the Christian, this is true of our adoption as children of God: we are reconciled to God through Christ and, therefore, in our call to work to bring about reconciliation in the world. We cannot abide with God if we are content to remain at loggerheads with other Christians.

In truth, the excuses we construct and with which we collude are very often designed to allow our own preferences to prevail. As we have seen over the past two weeks, separation is often an easier reality with which to live. Paul will have none of it. To be a new creation is to model the very thing that made us so! Reconciling Christians are not distinctive, therefore, but typical. If this is the biblical standard and template, what does it mean for you and for your fellowship?

Prayer

God of all newness, you made us one with you in Jesus; may we see each other as children of the one true God and live the life which speaks of a better and stronger unity. For his sake. Amen

Andrew John

Risk and opportunity

Then I saw 'a new heaven and a new earth,' for the first heaven and the first earth had passed away, and there was no longer any sea. I saw the Holy City, the new Jerusalem, coming down out of heaven from God, prepared as a bride beautifully dressed for her husband. And I heard a loud voice from the throne saying, 'Look! God's dwelling-place is now among the people, and he will dwell with them. They will be his people, and God himself will be with them and be their God.'

Those reading these verses without a church background might hear strains of the theme from the film *Titanic*. As the great liner disappears beneath the waters, a priest reads the first lines of today's passage. It is a rather despairing setting for what is actually a very hopeful passage. No doubt the film gained some extra drama by including this touch of religious fervour, but the meaning of the verses was skewed by their context. John's vision points not to a doom-laden 'end' but to what God will accomplish in the end-times. The picture is one of harmony and unity and completed fellowship between God and his people. The sea (often a motif for anxiety in Jewish tradition) will be no more, no longer threatening the security God provides. This vision offers the encouragement that God will not be defeated. His good plans will one day come about.

All this should not distract us from the call we have received from God for our lifetimes. Quite the opposite: we are to work with God towards that great final 'day'. A church united and one with God is something we must strive for, because it is God's clear purpose. We must allow this vision to shape our current practices, generating different activities and new priorities. Our task is to align ourselves with God's good will now. Such an undertaking is risky and yet full of promise and opportunity.

Prayer

God of grace, praise to you for what you promise. Let your church respond with faith and ambition to share in your task. May we be one in Jesus, your Son and our Lord. Amen

ANDREW JOHN

2 Kings 13—17

It is probably safe to say that the latter chapters of 2 Kings are among the less well-known in the Bible. The colourful characters have gone— no more Solomons, Elijahs or Jezebels—and what we find is an apparently unending series of calamitous monarchs, set on leading their people to disaster. Our section (chapters 13—17) begins with bad King Jehoahaz of Israel and concludes with the downfall of what had been his kingdom at the hands of the Assyrians.

What can we learn from this litany of trouble, struggle and eventual catastrophe? In the Hebrew Bible (what Christians call the Old Testament), 1 and 2 Kings are the last of the former prophets (Joshua, Judges, Samuel, Kings) and these books present a particular—prophetic—view of history. They are prophetic not in the sense of foretelling the future but of laying bare the spiritual reality of a situation, the divine perspective on human affairs. In the stories of the books of Kings, the same pattern recurs: the people are disobedient; they suffer (often as a result of foreign invasion); they cry out to God who rescues them; national life is restored to peace and prosperity; the people are disobedient again. From a human perspective, the events may have seemed a haphazard sequence of troubles; from God's perspective, there was a clear chain of cause and effect.

Nowadays, we tend to judge governments primarily on how they handle the economy, but, when passing judgment on kings such as Jehoahaz, Amaziah, Azariah and Pekah, what mattered to the writers of Kings were their religious policies—whether they encouraged the worship of other gods or tolerated worship of the true God conducted outside Jerusalem. We only discover anything about contemporary social conditions via comments in other prophetic writings of the time. Imagine a history of 20th-century Britain written from such a standpoint!

As we read over the next two weeks, we must engage our imaginations to discern something of the human suffering behind the stark narrative. We must also open our hearts to learning more of the nature of God and his working in history, despite the grim nature of so many of those stories.

Naomi Starkey

Anger and mercy

Jehoahaz son of Jehu began to reign over Israel... The anger of the Lord was kindled against Israel, so that he gave them repeatedly into the hands of King Hazael of Aram, then into the hand of Ben-hadad son of Hazael. But Jehoahaz entreated the Lord, and the Lord heeded him; for he saw the oppression of Israel, how the king of Aram oppressed them. Therefore the Lord gave Israel a saviour, so that they escaped from the hand of the Arameans; and the people of Israel lived in their homes as formerly. Nevertheless they did not depart from the sins of the house of Jeroboam.

In this passage we see played out the chain of events outlined in the Introduction: disobedience (verse 2 tells how the king's sins led his entire people astray), disaster, pleas for mercy, salvation, restoration—and continued disobedience.

The phrase 'the anger of the Lord' may trouble us because we are used to thinking that our God is a God of love. We may be disturbed by ideas of an 'Angry Old Testament God', but the same Old Testament also tells us that God's anger is slow to kindle (Exodus 34:6–7). Further, today's story demonstrates divine mercy and pity just as much as anger. After all, Israel had been warned about keeping its side of God's covenant, with the dire consequences spelled out by prophet after prophet. Here, though, the very same king who 'did what was evil in the sight of the Lord' (2 Kings 13:2) entreats the Lord for deliverance—and, astonishingly, an unidentified 'saviour' is sent (v. 5). The people escape, then settle back home with sighs of relief. Nothing changes.

Reflecting on our own lives, we may be aware of times when God has acted to save us, perhaps even before we were aware that we needed saving. When we identify such times, are we open to learning whatever lessons he would have us learn?

Reflection

'Jerusalem... the city that kills the prophets and stones those who are sent to it! How often have I desired to gather your children together as a hen gathers her brood under her wings, and you were not willing!' (Luke 13:34).

Naomi Starkey

The benefit of hindsight

In the thirty-seventh year of King Joash of Judah, Jehoash son of Jehoahaz began to reign over Israel... Now when Elisha had fallen sick with the illness of which he was to die, King Joash of Israel went down to him, and wept before him, crying, 'My father, my father! The chariots of Israel and its horsemen!' Elisha said to him, '... The Lord's arrow of victory, the arrow of victory over Aram! For you shall fight the Arameans in Aphek until you have made an end of them'... So Elisha died and they buried him.

Here we say goodbye to Elisha, one of the last major Old Testament 'characters' whose personalities loom as large as their messages. The strange words that the king weeps over the dying man are the same as Elisha himself cried out as his 'father in God', Elijah, disappeared from view (2 Kings 2:12). Commentators are unsure whether they imply 'heavenly hosts' coming to collect the prophet or that the prophet was a strong defender of Israel. Either way, they reverberate with grief and loss.

In every generation, God gifts certain people with unusual powers of insight into the affairs of the world and the motivations of the human heart. Few would be happy to claim the title 'prophet' for themselves and rightly so, yet they undeniably have prophetic gifts. Their task is, as it has always been, to challenge the status quo, question assumptions and call the church to account—and they often get a hostile reception. Nobody likes their certainties shaken, especially those who are certain that their beliefs represent the only possible truth.

With hindsight, the God-given quality of these prophetic words may be recognised, even as their immediate challenge is diminished by the passage of time. The Israelite king in our passage (also known as Joash, confusingly) is recorded as having done 'evil in the sight of the Lord' (13:11). Is his grief as much for his own stubbornness in not heeding the prophet in his lifetime as for Elisha's imminent demise?

Reflection

Hindsight is a wonderful thing, but it is better to pray for courage here and now to acknowledge whatever prophetic insights may be presented to us.

Naomi Starkey

Limits on chaos

In the second year of King Joash... of Israel, King Amaziah son of Joash of Judah began to reign... He did what was right in the sight of the Lord, yet not like his ancestor David; in all things he did as his father Joash had done. But the high places were not removed; the people still sacrificed and made offerings on the high places. As soon as the royal power was firmly in his hand he killed his servants who had murdered his father the king. But he did not put to death the children of the murderers.

Here is a little relief in the catalogue of woeful rulers—but only a little. Amaziah of Judah 'did what was right', but he was not considered as good as David, the gold standard for kingship. In line with the agenda of the writers (identified by scholars as the 'Deuteronomistic historians', because their perspective is also evident in Deuteronomy), Amaziah's limitations are evident in the fact that he does not remove the 'high places'—unofficial altars used for worship rituals outside Jerusalem—and restrict worship to the temple.

Bizarrely, to our ears, he is cited as acting 'according to what is written in the book of the law of Moses' (v. 6) because he murders only the servants who killed his father and not their children. Is this yet another example of a horrible 'Old Testament God' advocating violence or, rather, should we note the fact that God's law *limited* retribution, in contrast to traditions that prevailed over many centuries in many imperial systems around the world?

It is interesting to reflect on the broad sweep of God's law in the light of Jesus' remark: 'Because of your hardness of heart he wrote this commandment for you' (Mark 10:5). The context for that remark was a challenge about divorce, but the point surely is that God's law so often provides for—or restricts—the chaos created by human sinfulness. In the world as God originally intended (and—as we are promised—it will be again, one day), such sinfulness will no longer have the power to mar relationships, whether between individuals or across society.

Reflection

O Lord, have mercy on us, miserable offenders...

NAOMI STARKEY

Battle bravado

Then Amaziah sent messengers to King Jehoash... of Israel, saying, 'Come, let us look one another in the face.' King Jehoash of Israel sent word to King Amaziah of Judah, '... You have indeed defeated Edom, and your heart has lifted you up. Be content with your glory, and stay at home; for why should you provoke trouble so that you fall, you and Judah with you?' But Amaziah would not listen. So King Jehoash of Israel went up; he and King Amaziah of Judah faced one another in battle... Judah was defeated by Israel; everyone fled home.

This story (do take a moment to read it in full) has a troubling air of playground swagger about it: 'I dare you... come and take me on—if you're hard enough!' Amaziah of Judah had already soundly defeated the Edomites (v. 7), but, as Jehoash (or Joash) of Israel points out, he seems to want to provoke trouble. What follows is catastrophic for Judah. The 'alpha males' face up to one another on the battlefield. They fight—Israel against Judah, cousin against cousin—and the kingdom of Judah and the city of Jerusalem are left broken and plundered.

Now, what was the point of that, boys?

So often, wars are later judged to have been waged for selfish or simply stupid motives. While rhetoric at the time may glorify a planned conflict, the cost in human suffering (whether intentional or 'collateral damage') is terrible. Some situations seem to argue for warfare as the lesser of two evils, but we should not forget that admitting such an argument still names war as evil. It is not good, not as God intended the world to be. Reading of war between Israel and Judah is particularly poignant in the light of how God's people were intended to live. God had warned, through the prophet Samuel, that becoming a monarchy would not improve the nation (1 Samuel 8); today's story reads like the sad coda to that warning. They got a king and what followed was conflict upon conflict.

Prayer

Lord God, we pray for your blessing and protection on all those who work for peace. Grace them with courage and perseverance in their task.

NAOMI STARKEY

Saved by a bad king

In the fifteenth year of King Amaziah... King Jeroboam son of Joash of Israel began to reign in Samaria... He restored the border of Israel... according to the word of the Lord, the God of Israel, which he spoke by his servant Jonah son of Amittai, the prophet, who was from Gath-hepher. For the Lord saw that the distress of Israel was very bitter; there was no one left, bond or free, and no one to help Israel. But the Lord had not said that he would blot out the name of Israel from under heaven, so he saved them by the hand of Jeroboam son of Joash.

In a single verse, another famous Old Testament character makes a fleeting appearance. This is the only reference to the prophet Jonah outside his book, with scholars making a case for the story of his trip to Nineveh being written later than 1 and 2 Kings, to teach specific lessons about God's mercy. Even so, it is intriguing to find this tiny snapshot of Jonah engaged in the prophetic task closer to home.

The prophets Amos and Hosea were contemporaries of Jeroboam and a glance at their books reveals something of the social and moral conditions of the times. Theirs was an economically divided society, the wealthy enjoying leisured luxury while the poor worked for a pittance. Does that ring any disturbingly contemporary bells?

Jeroboam of Israel (who is actually Jeroboam II, Jeroboam I having been the first ruler of Israel after the split with Judah: 1 Kings 12:20), is not cited as being a good king ('he did what was evil', 2 Kings 14:24), but, despite this, God uses him to deliver Israel from their 'bitter distress'. Just because we find God's blessing on our enterprise, we should not assume that all we do, think and say enjoys the same blessing. The purposes of God are beyond our comprehension; if we sense our part in the unfolding of those purposes, our response should be humility and gratitude. As Andrew John pointed out (see 16 January), we should never permit ourselves any arrogant 'God is on our side' assumptions.

Reflection
'So if you think you are standing, watch out that you do not fall'
(1 Corinthians 10:12).

NAOMI STARKEY

Anarchy rules

Shallum son of Jabesh began to reign in the thirty-ninth year of King Uzziah of Judah; he reigned one month in Samaria. Then Menahem son of Gadi came up from Tirzah and came to Samaria; he struck down Shallum son of Jabesh in Samaria and killed him; he reigned in place of him. Now the rest of the deeds of Shallum, including the conspiracy that he made, are written in the Book of the Annals of the Kings of Israel. At that time Menahem sacked Tiphsah, all who were in it and its territory from Tirzah on; because they did not open it to him, he sacked it.

We keep our focus on the kings of Israel here. Over in Jerusalem, (relatively) good King Amaziah of Judah had been murdered after a conspiracy (14:19), succeeded by his son Azariah (also known as Uzziah, 15:13 and see Isaiah 6:1). He reigned for 52 years, during which time the Samaria-based Israelite throne changed hands five times.

King Shallum is violently overthrown, just as he violently overthrew the previous king, Zechariah son of Jeroboam II, who had reigned for just six months (2 Kings 15:8–10). Shallum's reign has an even briefer span—a single month—and Menahem, the brutal warlord who succeeds him, has a record of such atrocity that I could not bear to include the final part of verse 16 in today's reading. Like a virus, violence rages across the lands. The only true king now is Anarchy.

Thanks to the worldwide web of communications, we have no excuse for ignorance: there are still far too many parts of the world where the rule of law is non-existent, where might is always right, where the loudest, harshest voices drown out all else. God's command to his people was 'you shall love your neighbour as yourself' (Leviticus 19:18). If 'neighbours' are those with whom we can be in daily contact, then these days we cannot plead geographical distance in mitigation of our lack of love and care for the most vulnerable in our world.

Prayer

Lord God, give us compassionate hearts—and eyes to see where and how you call us to show that compassion.

NAOMI STARKEY

Desperate times

In the thirty-ninth year of King Azariah of Judah, Menahem son of Gadi began to reign over Israel; he reigned ten years in Samaria. He did what was evil in the sight of the Lord... King Pul of Assyria came against the land; Menahem gave Pul a thousand talents of silver, so that he might help him confirm his hold on the royal power. Menahem exacted the money from Israel, that is, from all the wealthy, fifty shekels of silver from each one, to give to the king of Assyria. So the king of Assyria turned back, and did not stay there in the land.

We are nearing the end of the northern kingdom. The menace of Assyria appears over the horizon and the nation that once relied on the Lord God to save them from their enemies is reduced to begging for piles of silver to pay off the aggressive foreign power. We can get some idea of the amount of silver involved by the fact that a single talent weighed around 33kg.

It can be disconcerting to realise how relatively insignificant both Israel and Judah were in the wider context of the ancient Near East. Israel's situation was desperate: it was a tiny monarchy facing the might of Pul, also known as Tiglath-Pileser III, who ruled as king of both Assyria and Babylon. Visitors to the British Museum in London can look at his likeness in stone—a military conqueror, administrative reformer, imperial potentate. By contrast, being God's people did not involve becoming any kind of superpower.

Working to extend God's kingdom on earth does not—and never should—result in empire-building. As Jesus taught his followers and Paul underlined to the new Christians in Corinth, God's power is all about servanthood, weakness and suffering. When we forget that, and when we act as if it is all about our own strength, influence and power, things will inevitably, eventually, start to go wrong.

Reflection

'So, I will boast all the more gladly of my weaknesses, so that the power of Christ may dwell in me. Therefore I am content with weaknesses, insults, hardships, persecutions, and calamities for the sake of Christ; for whenever I am weak, then I am strong' (2 Corinthians 12:9–10).

NAOMI STARKEY

Into exile

In the fifty-second year of King Azariah of Judah, Pekah son of
Remaliah began to reign over Israel in Samaria; he reigned twenty
years... King Tiglath-pileser of Assyria came and captured Ijon,
Abel-beth-maacah, Janoah, Kedesh, Hazor, Gilead, and Galilee,
all the land of Naphtali; and he carried the people captive to
Assyria. Then Hoshea son of Elah made a conspiracy against
Pekah son of Remaliah, attacked him, and killed him; he reigned
in place of him, in the twentieth year of Jotham son of Uzziah.

The throne of Israel changes hands for the fifth time, while King Azariah/
Uzziah is still on the throne of Judah. The new Israelite king is Pekah,
son of royal military captain Remaliah, who wrests power from Pekahiah,
the son of Menahem, after a mere two-year reign. Pekah himself manages
20 years, but they are hardly a triumph. Not only does he do 'evil' in
God's sight (v. 28) but Menahem's policy of paying off Assyria is shown
to have failed spectacularly. Tiglath-Pileser returns, captures a string of
settlements and territory and deports the people to Assyria. The
descendants of the people rescued from slavery in the exodus are now
forcibly removed and taken on a new journey into captivity—the exile.
Presumably in response to such disaster, Pekah is overthrown and murdered by Hoshea, who turns out to be the very last king of Israel.

Tales of Assyrian brutality are, some say, exaggerated, but even setting
aside deliberate acts of torture and humiliation, the trauma of deportation should not be underestimated. Resettling entire populations was a
feature of Stalinist policy during and after World War II, resulting in
countless deaths. Critics of Christianity will hold up examples of wicked-
ness perpetrated in the name of the church, such as the Crusades and
the Spanish Inquisition. What is sadly clear from even the briefest survey
of history is that humanity's capacity for cruelty seems limitless.

Reflection

*It is the work of 21st-century prophetic preachers... to name the despair
and to witness to the divine resolve for newness that may break the vicious
cycles of self-destruction and make new common life possible.*

Walter Brueggemann, *The Practice of Prophetic Imagination* (Fortress, 2012)

NAOMI STARKEY

A very bad king

In the seventeenth year of Pekah son of Remaliah, King Ahaz son of Jotham of Judah began to reign... He did not do what was right in the sight of the Lord his God, as his ancestor David had done, but he walked in the way of the kings of Israel. He even made his son pass through fire, according to the abominable practices of the nations whom the Lord drove out before the people of Israel. He sacrificed and made offerings on the high places, on the hills, and under every green tree.

Time now for a catch-up on what had been happening in the southern kingdom of Judah. King Azariah/Uzziah finally died, two years after his golden jubilee, although, as he was suffering from leprosy (15:5), his son Jotham took charge in the final stages of his reign. Like his father, Jotham was judged as having done 'right in the eyes of the Lord', but still was not determined enough to rid the country of the old worship sites (15:34–35). Compared to its northern neighbour, Judah seemed to be in a place of at least some stability and at least adequate leadership, but then the throne passed to Ahaz.

Note that this is 'Ahaz', not 'Ahab' of Israel, who appears in 1 Kings and tussles with Elijah. Ahaz of Judah not only 'walked in the ways of the kings of Israel' (v. 3)—not a compliment—but also led the further fragmentation of worship and, worse still, even seems to have conducted child sacrifice (a practice also mentioned in 3:27).

Leadership, whether of an organisation, community, church or nation, does so much to set the tone for the lives of the people who are, in many ways, in that leadership's care. In a country where getting to the top means being able to drain the economy to fill your and your family's bank accounts, for example, honesty is hardly commended to the wider population. Power is a dangerous, potentially toxic brew— and unlimited power should mean unlimited responsibility, not unlimited venality.

Prayer

Lord God, grant grace and honesty to our governments and wise insight to all with the charisma of leadership.

NAOMI STARKEY

Your servant and your son

Then King Rezin of Aram and King Pekah son of Remaliah of Israel came up to wage war on Jerusalem; they besieged Ahaz but could not conquer him. At that time the king of Edom recovered Elath for Edom, and drove the Judeans from Elath... Ahaz sent messengers to King Tiglath-pileser of Assyria, saying, 'I am your servant and your son. Come up and rescue me...' Ahaz also took the silver and gold found in the house of the Lord and in the treasures of the king's house, and sent a present to the king of Assyria. The king of Assyria listened to him; the king of Assyria marched up against Damascus, and took it, carrying its people captive to Kir.

'Aram' is another name for Syria (the capital of which, Damascus, is recorded here as conquered). Syria and Israel had joined in an unsuccessful attack on Judah, also mentioned in Isaiah 7:1–17 and Hosea 5:8–15, where the prophet warns of the danger of accepting Assyrian help (as well as in 2 Chronicles 28, both books of Chronicles offering their own take on events recounted in 1 and 2 Kings).

Ahaz's words to Tiglath-Pileser read as deeply ironic. Time and again the Old Testament uses the words 'servant' and 'son' to refer to the relationship between the Lord God and his chosen people, but here they are used in grovelling appeal, combined with a reckless ransacking of the temple and the king's own treasury, not even selling but giving away the family silver (and gold). Ahaz wins a reprieve for Judah, but only for the short term.

There is no mention of him crying out to the Lord for deliverance as he struggles to shore up the crumbling borders of his kingdom. Sadly, the further we walk from God, the harder we can find it to return, even when we most need to do so. If our wrongful actions unleash chaos, that chaos may well run its course, no matter how fervently we then repent and call for heavenly help.

Reflection

'See, the Lord's hand is not too short to save, nor his ear too dull to hear. Rather, your iniquities have been barriers between you and your God'
(Isaiah 59:1–2).

Naomi Starkey

Multitude of sacrifices

The priest Uriah built the altar; in accordance with all that King Ahaz had sent from Damascus... The king drew near to the altar, went up on it, and offered his burnt offering and his grain offering, poured his drink offering, and dashed the blood of his offerings of well-being against the altar... King Ahaz commanded the priest Uriah, saying, 'Upon the great altar offer the morning burnt offering, and the evening grain offering, and the king's burnt offering, and his grain offering, with the burnt offering of all the people of the land, their grain offering, and their drink offering... but the bronze altar shall be for me to inquire by.'

The context for today's passage is King Ahaz's visit to the Assyrian king in Damascus (v. 10), where he decides that the Jerusalem temple must have an identical altar to the one there. Uriah obliges, copying the model sent by Ahaz, who later (vv. 17–18) rearranges and remakes some of the other temple furnishings, 'because of the king of Assyria' (v. 18). Perhaps this work indicates his new, subject status, needing to placate his imperial overlord.

The passage is notable for its details of the routine sacrifices offered by both the king and the people of Judah. The Hebrew phrase for 'offering of well-being' used to be translated 'peace offering'. It involved burning part of the sacrificial animal, giving part to the priests and feasting on the rest. The burnt (animal) and grain offerings were burned entirely.

The king tells Uriah that he will use the old bronze altar to 'inquire by' (v. 15). This probably refers to divination—looking for good and bad omens by examining animal entrails, a practice banned in Deuteronomy 18:10–12, along with making children 'pass through fire', which Ahaz has also done. He seems to be keeping up the sacrificial system but ignoring the bigger problem—that he is far from God, struggling to save himself and his kingdom by his own feeble efforts.

Reflection

'What to me is the multitude of your sacrifices? ... When you stretch out your hands, I will hide my eyes from you; even though you make many prayers, I will not listen; your hands are full of blood' (Isaiah 1:11, 15).

NAOMI STARKEY

The bitter end for Israel

In the twelfth year of King Ahaz of Judah, Hoshea son of Elah began to reign in Samaria... King Shalmaneser of Assyria came up against him; Hoshea became his vassal, and paid him tribute. But the king of Assyria found treachery in Hoshea; for he had sent messengers to King So of Egypt, and offered no tribute to the king of Assyria... therefore the king of Assyria confined him and imprisoned him. Then the king of Assyria invaded all the land and came to Samaria; for three years he besieged it. In the ninth year of Hoshea the king of Assyria captured Samaria; he carried the Israelites away to Assyria.

Thus, the end comes. Hoshea has foolishly conspired with Egypt against Shalmaneser (son of Tiglath-Pileser) of Assyria, so he is punished and Samaria besieged. Assyrian inscriptions record that, by the time the three-year siege ended, the Assyrian conqueror was Sargon II, successor to Shalmaneser, and the people of Israel had been deported hundreds of miles, into the heart of their enemy's empire. The books of Nehemiah and Ezra tell how the people of Judah were later permitted to return from their own period of exile, but such permission was never granted to those from Israel. Speculation about the 'lost ten tribes of Israel' continues to this day, with communities across the world claiming to be their descendants (adherents of British Israelism, for example, believing that the British royal family are directly descended from King David).

As a result of the exile, the question reverberating across the Old Testament is 'How could this happen to God's own people?' What did the exodus and the promised land mean now? A theological reason is provided in tomorrow's passage, but today we have the political/military explanation. Hoshea gambled on an alliance with Egypt and lost, in a reversal of David and Goliath and so many other biblical stories in which victory is won against the odds because of reliance on divine—rather than human—guidance and protection.

Prayer

Lord God, we pray for all those who feel, for whatever reason, exiled and far from home. In your mercy, may they find their home in you.

NAOMI STARKEY

Reasons

This occurred because the people of Israel had sinned against the Lord their God, who had brought them up out of the land of Egypt from under the hand of Pharaoh king of Egypt. They had worshipped other gods and walked in the customs of the nations whom the Lord drove out before the people of Israel… Judah also did not keep the commandments of the Lord their God but walked in the customs that Israel had introduced. The Lord rejected all the descendants of Israel; he punished them and gave them into the hand of plunderers, until he had banished them from his presence.

The historians of 2 Kings spell out with painful clarity why events unfolded as they did, pointing out that the cause was rooted in the aftermath of the exodus. Israel chose to follow Canaanite religious practices, offering their worship elsewhere than to the God who had delivered them. Why had no one fully heeded the warnings of the prophets, delivered over so many years? Surely now Judah would learn from the northern kingdom's downfall and choose a better way? The rest of 2 Kings, however, tells the sad tale of the end of the southern kingdom, prefigured here in the judgment that the people persisted in the same wrongful ways as Israel.

We may shake our heads at such folly, but we, too, often persist with our own misguided plans instead of stilling ourselves to tune into God's priorities. We write our own life scripts, scheming for our desired outcomes, then we are shocked if things turn out very differently, perhaps disastrously. The stronger and more capable we think we are, the more tempting it is to believe that our way, our perspective, is the only right way, the only true perspective. We may forget all about listening, waiting, trusting—right up until our circumstances force us to remember.

Reflection

Prophetic preaching in our time and place fundamentally faces the reality of loss among us that dominant imagination could never, in its wildest imagination, imagine… It is about breaking the code of invulnerability that we had so deeply trusted.

Walter Brueggemann, *The Practice of Prophetic Imagination* (Fortress, 2012)

NAOMI STARKEY

Seeking hope

The king of Assyria brought people from Babylon… and placed them in the cities of Samaria in place of the people of Israel… When they first settled there, they did not worship the Lord; therefore the Lord sent lions among them, which killed some of them… Then the king of Assyria commanded, 'Send there one of the priests whom you carried away from there; let him go and live there, and teach them the law of the god of the land.' So one of the priests whom they had carried away from Samaria came and lived in Bethel; he taught them how they should worship the Lord.

Here is the final outworking of the Assyrian imperial policies. Sargon II resettles the more-or-less emptied land of Israel (scholarly opinion differs on the extent of the deportation) with new inhabitants from elsewhere. The land promised to the descendants of Abraham is now given, at least in part, into the hands of others.

This is a challenging episode (setting aside what it means that 'the Lord sent lions' to kill those not practising a religion they had not been taught) because it reminds us that God's agenda is far greater than we understand. His chosen people turned away from him, so they lost their promised land, new people were settled there and they were taught to worship him. Sadly, though, the rest of the chapter explains that the new inhabitants were also unfaithful and disobedient. If we were God, we might have been tempted to give up on the whole human race enterprise, which had generated nothing but grief and bloodshed.

We have already seen in these passages, however, that the kingdom of God is not characterised by the dynamics of empire-building. The hope represented by the promise of God's kingdom is manifest most often at the grassroots of life. No matter how comprehensive the devastation, how strong the sense that the entire ground of our being has been concreted over and rendered sterile, the green shoots of God's life can still break through.

Reflection

We believe in an eternal, loving God, so there is always hope, even if we struggle to understand what that means in our present circumstances.

NAOMI STARKEY

Bible stories rediscovered:
Queen Esther

For the next fortnight our readings will be from the book of Esther. It is one of only two biblical books named after a woman and it is the only book in the whole of the Bible that fails even to mention God, forgiveness, worship or prayer. Perhaps that is why it was long argued over, in terms of its place in the canon of scripture.

You may be wondering why on earth we should bother to read such a book in *New Daylight*. The answer is that Esther only reveals her jewels of enlightenment, challenge and insight to those who are prepared to look beneath the surface of what is, by any standards, a colourful and exciting story. Many scholars call it a 'diaspora novella', which is their way of saying that it is a story—or perhaps a parable, probably with an historical foundation—that was written to raise the morale of an alien religious minority living in the world's most powerful empire. It is also the biblical justification for the noisy and raucous feast of Purim, which Jews everywhere celebrate over two days in March or April every year. Like the book itself, Purim is not very 'religious'!

Esther is set in the days of King Ahasuerus, otherwise known as Xerxes I, who ruled the massive empire of Persia in the fifth century BC. The empire included a substantial Jewish community, many of them descendants of people taken there as slaves in the previous century but now living and working peacefully as what today we would call an 'ethnic minority'. The story involves that minority facing genocide, but then seeing the whole situation turned around so that a Jewish leader, Mordecai, became second only to Ahasuerus in his court. Shades of Joseph in Egypt and Daniel in Babylon!

Esther is a brilliantly told story that, at a deeper level, is about two things, human power and divine providence. The fact the source of that providence is never named in the book makes it more, not less, intriguing.

David Winter

ESTHER 1:2–7 (NRSV, ABRIDGED)

Splendour and pomp

In those days when King Ahasuerus sat on his royal throne in the citadel of Susa, in the third year of his reign, he gave a banquet for all his officials and ministers. The army of Persia and Media and the nobles and governors of the provinces were present, while he displayed the great wealth of his kingdom and the splendour and pomp of his majesty for many days, one hundred and eighty days in all. When these days were completed, the king gave for all the people present in the citadel of Susa, both great and small, a banquet lasting for seven days, in the court of the garden of the king's palace... There were couches of gold and silver on a mosaic pavement of porphyry, marble, mother-of-pearl, and coloured stones. Drinks were served in golden goblets, goblets of different kinds, and the royal wine was lavished according to the bounty of the king.

The story that is to follow is here put in its setting—one of unbelievable power, wealth and indulgence. These are the greatest days of the mighty Persian Empire and Ahasuerus, the king, lives in splendour and pomp in his palace in Susa. The writer describes it with more than a hint of hyperbole—surely even the most indulgent monarch would not hold a banquet that lasted six months! Not only that but he also arranged a second banquet to which everyone was invited, 'great and small'.

The details also speak of indulgence and wealth—golden goblets, a pavement of porphyry, marble and mother of pearl and gold and silver couches. What more could you ask?

Banquets feature a lot in this story (there are more of them in Esther than in all the rest of the Bible)—occasions of feasting and fellowship, but also occasions to be reminded of the glories of the empire and the king's power. As we shall see, however, the empire also had a less 'glorious' side and the king's power was about to be challenged in an unexpected way.

Reflection

A banquet celebrating the glory of the kingdom may have a previous echo in Jewish thought (and in Christian faith) in the great messianic banquet of the Lamb (Revelation 19:9). 'Small and great' welcome!

DAVID WINTER

Power without respect

Furthermore, Queen Vashti gave a banquet for the women in the palace of King Ahasuerus. On the seventh day, when the king was merry with wine, he commanded... the seven eunuchs who attended him to bring Queen Vashti before the king, wearing the royal crown, in order to show the peoples and the officials her beauty; for she was fair to behold. But Queen Vashti refused to come at the king's command conveyed by the eunuchs. At this the king was enraged, and his anger burned within him. Then the king consulted the sages who knew the laws... 'According to the law, what is to be done to Queen Vashti because she has not performed the command of King Ahasuerus conveyed by the eunuchs?'

While the king was having his male banquet, his queen was entertaining her female friends and courtiers at a separate celebration in the palace. A week into the festivities, 'when the king was merry with wine' (v. 10), he decided to give his guests a real treat. He sent his eunuchs to command Queen Vashti to attend his banquet and show off her beauty to the 'the peoples and the officials' (v. 11). It was, by any standards, an awful idea, treating his wife and queen as though she were an exhibit, and showed an appalling lack of respect for her as a person and as his consort.

Bravely, she refused to attend. Shockwaves ran through the palace. The king, who all through this story comes across as weak and vacillating, was taken aback by her response. 'What should I do?' he demanded of his advisers. He had clearly lost face (a terrible thing for a monarch) and his authority had been challenged.

Most present-day readers will be cheering for Vashti. She had been treated disgracefully by her husband. Even the absolute power of a monarch in the ancient world did not excuse such wilful disrespect. By her refusal, she had avoided public humiliation, but in the process she had undermined the authority of Ahasuerus. What next?

Reflection
Respect is a dignity we are to accord to everyone made in the image of God, whether they are queens or rough sleepers.

DAVID WINTER

Master in his house

[Memucan the official] said, '… This deed of the queen will be made known to all women, causing them to look with contempt on their husbands, since they will say, "King Ahasuerus commanded Queen Vashti to be brought before him, and she did not come." This very day the noble ladies of Persia and Media who have heard of the queen's behaviour will rebel against the king's officials, and there will be no end of contempt and wrath! If it pleases the king, let a royal order go out from him… that Vashti is never again to come before King Ahasuerus; and let the king give her royal position to another who is better than she. So when the decree made by the king is proclaimed throughout all his kingdom, vast as it is, all women will give honour to their husbands, high and low alike.'… The king did as Memucan proposed; he sent letters to all the royal provinces… declaring that every man should be master in his own house.

So here we see a weak but also powerful king being persuaded by his advisers that the reaction of Queen Vashti to his demeaning order was likely to cause a wave of domestic disobedience by the ladies of the Persian empire. The superiority and leadership status of men in general would be challenged and anarchy would reign in every home: no end of contempt (by the women) and no end of wrath (on the male side). Readers may appreciate the relevance of this spat to certain debates going on in church circles today!

For Vashti, it meant the end of her reign; even her beauty could not save her. Her dismissal, however, was to be covered up under the guise of a general commandment (the law of the Medes and Persians, which could not be changed: v. 19) that 'every man should be master in his own house'. Meanwhile, the search would begin for a new queen.

Reflection

The storyteller is setting up a situation in which, whatever the king's commandment was, the shape of events would, in fact, be determined by a young woman, at present unknown to the royal court of Persia.

DAVID WINTER

Applications invited

After these things, when the anger of King Ahasuerus had abated, he remembered Vashti and what she had done and what had been decreed against her. Then the king's servants who attended him said, 'Let beautiful young virgins be sought out for the king. And let the king appoint commissioners in all the provinces of his kingdom to gather all the beautiful young virgins to the harem in the citadel of Susa under custody of Hegai, the king's eunuch, who is in charge of the women; let their cosmetic treatments be given them. And let the girl who pleases the king be queen instead of Vashti.' This pleased the king, and he did so.

If the original treatment of Queen Vashti was demeaning, what is the modern reader likely to make of the method used to choose her successor outlined in our passage today? The court officials, now flushed with their new authority, will be sent off on a kind of beauty hunt, to find and bring to the capital the most attractive virgins they can find. Once there, and in the care of the keeper of the harem, they would be given 'cosmetic treatments' (presumably the application of lotions and perfumes and probably a 'free-from-infection' test) lasting twelve months (vv. 10–14). Finally, the chosen few would each sleep with the king for one night, so that he could choose the one who 'pleased' him best. It is not difficult to imagine the kinds of favours the officials might have demanded of the candidates. The fact that all of this was quite normal in the world of the time does not make it any less humiliating for the women involved.

What is surprising—and this is the next twist in the plot—is that this tortuous and demeaning process would eventually produce not only an outstanding queen but also a woman who would outwit the cunning of the cleverest courtiers and, in the process, rescue multitudes of people from disaster.

Reflection

'Providence'—the protective care of God in the face of future eventualities—is about to take a hand in events in the kingdom of Ahasuerus, even events as bizarre and distasteful as these.

DAVID WINTER

'There was a Jew'

Now there was a Jew in the citadel of Susa whose name was Mordecai son of Jair son of Shimei son of Kish, a Benjaminite... Mordecai had brought up Hadassah, that is Esther, his cousin, for she had neither father nor mother; the girl was fair and beautiful, and when her father and her mother died, Mordecai adopted her as his own daughter. So when the king's order and his edict were proclaimed, and when many young women were gathered in the citadel of Susa in custody of Hegai, Esther also was taken into the king's palace and put in custody of Hegai, who had charge of the women. The girl pleased him and won his favour, and he quickly provided her with her cosmetic treatments and her portion of food, and with seven chosen maids from the king's palace, and advanced her and her maids to the best place in the harem. Esther did not reveal her people or kindred, for Mordecai had charged her not to tell.

'There was a Jew'—ah, so that is what this story is all about! Mordecai was of the tribe of Benjamin (a detail that becomes significant later), a descendant of the Jews who had been taken into captivity in the Persian Empire under Nebuchadnezzar a century earlier. As time passed, the Jews settled in the land, no longer as captives but as alien citizens, a religious and ethnic minority who survived by being discreet and law-abiding.

Mordecai had a ward—the beautiful Esther (or Hadassah, to use her Jewish name). He was actually her cousin, but 'adopted' her when her parents died. A shrewd man, perhaps he saw that a place in the court of Ahasuerus might be a notable advantage to the Jewish minority and so encouraged her to join the candidates for the crown vacated by Vashti. The 'fair and beautiful' Esther was an immediate hit with the master of the harem, Hegai, who immediately gave her considerable privileges. He did not, however, know that she was Jewish. Following Mordecai's instructions, Esther kept quiet about that.

Reflection

As so often, the unfolding of God's providential purpose is slow but sure.

DAVID WINTER

Queen Esther

When the turn came for Esther daughter of Abihail the uncle of Mordecai, who had adopted her as his own daughter, to go in to the king, she asked for nothing except what Hegai the king's eunuch, who had charge of the women, advised. Now Esther was admired by all who saw her. When Esther was taken to King Ahasuerus in his royal palace in the tenth month, which is the month of Tebeth, in the seventh year of his reign, the king loved Esther more than all the other women; of all the virgins she won his favour and devotion, so that he set the royal crown on her head and made her queen instead of Vashti. Then the king gave a great banquet to all his officials and ministers—'Esther's banquet'.

So, on the evidence of one night, and possibly the advice of Hegai, the warden of the harem, Ahasuerus made his choice. Of the hundreds of young girls he might have chosen, Esther, the young Jewish woman, was to become queen. The storyteller seems to be emphasising her modesty: she simply followed Hegai's advice and asked for nothing beyond the normal treatment.

She won the king's heart so completely that the selection process came to an abrupt halt and the crown was placed on her head. Mordecai, we are told, 'Every day... would walk around in front of the court of the harem, to learn how Esther was and how she fared' (v. 11). He must have felt that his stratagem had worked well because, throughout all this, Esther had carefully followed his instructions and had not revealed 'her kindred or her people' (v. 20). The mighty empire of Persia now had a Jewish queen, but the king was not aware of it. Needless to say, those two facts are elements further on in this slowly unfolding and intriguing story.

Reflection

The Persian Empire included people of many races, languages and cultures, so Mordecai's decision to keep Esther's 'kindred' secret would probably not have been through fear of prejudice. His caution, however, was to prove a vital part of the providential process by means of which evil power was to be frustrated. Sometimes silence is golden!

DAVID WINTER

A loyal subject

When the virgins were being gathered together, Mordecai was sitting at the king's gate… In those days, while Mordecai was sitting at the king's gate, Bigthan and Teresh, two of the king's eunuchs, who guarded the threshold, became angry and conspired to assassinate King Ahasuerus. But the matter came to the knowledge of Mordecai, and he told it to Queen Esther, and Esther told the king in the name of Mordecai. When the affair was investigated and found to be so, both the men were hanged on the gallows. It was recorded in the book of the annals in the presence of the king.

We already know that Mordecai spent hours hanging around near the palace and especially the harem, keeping an eye on Esther's welfare. However, while he was there, he also picked up some highly valuable information. Two of the king's eunuchs had become angry with the king and were plotting to assassinate him. One might think that a member of an alien minority, once enslaved in the land, would not feel any great loyalty to the regime, but Mordecai decided to pass this information on to the king, by way of his adopted daughter, the queen. From what we learn of his character in this book, we may assume that he did this not only out of a sense of civic duty but also out of political shrewdness. It would do no harm to the Jewish cause, if things got difficult, to have it recorded that a prominent Jew helped to save the king's life. Mordecai's deed was duly noted in the 'book of the annals' (as well as feasts, written records also feature prominently in Esther) and the two would-be assassins were hanged on the gallows.

It seems a relatively small incident, but, in this carefully plotted story, no detail is insignificant, as we shall see. An enemy of the Jewish people is about to appear on the scene and the defence of their freedom will require every ounce of shrewdness and every possible political alliance they can fashion.

Reflection

Even if our motives are at times mixed, doing the right thing
is still doing the right thing!

DAVID WINTER

No other Lord

After these things King Ahasuerus promoted Haman son of Hammedatha the Agagite... and set his seat above all the officials who were with him. And all the king's servants who were at the king's gate bowed down and did obeisance to Haman; for the king had so commanded concerning him. But Mordecai did not bow down or do obeisance. Then the king's servants who were at the king's gate said to Mordecai, 'Why do you disobey the king's command?' When they spoke to him... they told Haman, in order to see whether Mordecai's words would avail; for he had told them that he was a Jew. When Haman saw that Mordecai did not bow down or do obeisance to him, Haman was infuriated. But he thought it beneath him to lay hands on Mordecai alone. So, having been told who Mordecai's people were, Haman plotted to destroy all the Jews, the people of Mordecai, throughout the whole kingdom of Ahasuerus.

Now we meet the villain, Haman the Agagite. The tribal reference is significant. Mordecai was a distant descendant of Saul, the first king of Israel (Kish was Saul's father, 1 Samuel 9:3). Haman was a member of the tribe of Agag, deadly enemies of Saul (1 Samuel 15:8). As we say today, they had 'form'! So, there was bound to be trouble when Ahasuerus promoted Haman above all the other officials in his court and commanded his servants to bow down in his presence.

As we have already seen, Mordecai was in the habit of loitering outside the palace where Esther was now the queen. This meant that whenever Haman passed by, everyone would notice that he did not bow down to him. This may have been on religious grounds or possibly out of loyalty to his ancestors and their historic feuds with the people of Agag. The other servants were told by Mordecai that he did not bow 'because he was a Jew'. Haman, outraged at this blatant show of disrespect, determined to make every Jew living in the empire suffer as a result. His intention was nothing less than genocide.

Reflection

'It is written, "Worship the Lord your God, and serve only him"'
(Matthew 4:10).

DAVID WINTER

Haman's vengeance

Haman said to King Ahasuerus, 'There is a certain people scattered and separated among the peoples in all the provinces of your kingdom; their laws are different from those of every other people, and they do not keep the king's laws, so that it is not appropriate for the king to tolerate them. If it pleases the king, let a decree be issued for their destruction, and I will pay ten thousand talents of silver... into the king's treasuries.' So the king took his signet ring and gave it to Haman son of Hammedatha the Agagite, the enemy of the Jews... Letters were sent by couriers to all the king's provinces, giving orders to destroy, to kill, and to annihilate all Jews, young and old, women and children, in one day, the thirteenth day of the twelfth month, which is the month of Adar... When Mordecai learned all that had been done, Mordecai tore his clothes and put on sackcloth and ashes, and went through the city, wailing with a loud and bitter cry.

This is exactly how racial prejudice works. Look at the way Haman describes the Jews, hitherto law-abiding and peaceful members of the kingdom. They are different. They are separated. They live by other values. So 'it is not appropriate for them to be tolerated'.

Obviously up to this point Ahasuerus was not aware of these dangerous dissidents in his kingdom—much less that he was married to one of them! Weak, greedy, gullible, he handed over the signet ring of his authority to Haman and the dreadful decree became law. The date was fixed—Haman arranged the casting of lots for it (v. 7)—and Mordecai, perhaps horrified at the consequences of his very minor act of defiance, wept and grieved through the streets of the city.

This kind of prejudice, based largely on fear of 'difference' (the literal meaning of 'xenophobia'), has often been the lot of minority groups. It was in much the same language that Roman emperors denounced the early Christians. Add to it, as here, a personal vendetta and the mix is both evil and deadly.

Reflection

May God help us to respect the beauty and dignity of difference—
Jew, Gentile, slave, free, male, female... (Galatians 3:28).

DAVID WINTER

For such a time as this

Then Esther spoke to Hathach and gave him a message for Mordecai, saying, 'All the king's servants and the people of the king's provinces know that if any man or woman goes to the king inside the inner court without being called, there is but one law—all alike are to be put to death. Only if the king holds out the golden sceptre to someone, may that person live. I myself have not been called to come in to the king for thirty days.' When they told Mordecai what Esther had said, Mordecai told them to reply to Esther, 'Do not think that in the king's palace you will escape any more than all the other Jews. For if you keep silence at such a time as this, relief and deliverance will rise for the Jews from another quarter, but you and your father's family will perish. Who knows? Perhaps you have come to royal dignity for just such a time as this.'

Mordecai, desperate to find a way to save the Jews of the Persian Empire, has asked Esther to petition the king on their behalf (vv. 7–8), but, as she points out here, even the queen is not allowed to initiate an audience with Ahasuerus. Death was the penalty for approaching him uninvited.

When her message reaches Mordecai, his reply is uncompromising. Esther must not think that she, a Jew, will be safe simply because she dwells in the royal palace. How can she keep silent? We then find for the first time an oblique reference to an anonymous other who will guard the interests of the Jews: 'relief and deliverance will rise... from another quarter' (v. 14). What is that 'quarter' if not the God of Abraham, Isaac and Jacob? Perhaps the author knows that this story will be circulated within Persia and discretion may best serve their cause.

The same anonymous other is hinted at in Mordecai's final words to Esther here: 'Perhaps you have come to royal dignity for such a time as this' (v. 14). A purpose comes from somewhere—divine providence is at work.

Reflection

Responsibilities can be accepted and opportunities seized—
'for such a time as this'.

DAVID WINTER

If I perish, I perish

Then Esther said in reply to Mordecai, 'Go, gather all the Jews to be found in Susa, and hold a fast on my behalf, and neither eat nor drink for three days, night or day. I and my maids will also fast as you do. After that I will go to the king, though it is against the law; and if I perish, I perish.' Mordecai then went away and did everything as Esther had ordered him.

The beautiful queen is here revealed as a woman of courage and cool determination. Perhaps Mordecai's words had stung her. Perhaps she had only just begun to grasp both the imminence of the disaster facing her fellow Jews and the influence she might be able to wield with her husband. Her human pleas needed something more, however. Surely the request for three days of fasting by the Jews would necessarily include prayer (again, the secrecy code seems to be applied). Instead of going into hiding, the people will turn to their anonymous other, the God of Israel.

When the days of fasting are over, Queen Esther will go to the king (despite the fact that she was forbidden to do so uninvited). She has weighed up the consequences and puts them starkly: 'if I perish, I perish' (v. 16). The change from her earlier stance is striking. Suddenly the king's authority is less crucial than the survival of her people.

Mordecai received her message and 'did everything as Esther had ordered him' (v. 17). Again, what a change! Until now, Esther had carefully done whatever her guardian told her to do. Now suddenly the boot is on the other foot, with Esther giving the orders and Mordecai ensuring that they are carried out—and this in a land where the king had ordered that every man should be master in his house!

However, the edict ordering the annihilation of the Jews is still in force and Haman, their implacable enemy, is still second only to the king in power. We will see next what prayer and fasting can do in the face of that.

Reflection
'If I perish, I perish' is the cry of all those willing to sacrifice their own lives for the sake of others.

DAVID WINTER

Loyalty vindicated

On that night the king could not sleep, and he gave orders to bring the book of records, the annals, and they were read to the king. It was found written how Mordecai had told about Bigthana and Teresh, two of the king's eunuchs, who guarded the threshold, and who had conspired to assassinate King Ahasuerus. Then the king said, 'What honour or distinction has been bestowed on Mordecai for this?' The king's servants who attended him said, 'Nothing has been done for him.' The king said, 'Who is in the court?' Now Haman had just entered the outer court of the king's palace to speak to the king about having Mordecai hanged on the gallows that he had prepared for him. So the king's servants told him, 'Haman is there, standing in the court.' The king said, 'Let him come in.'

Once again the anonymous other is at work! The king cannot sleep, so asks for the book of records to be read to him (better than counting sheep). He then discovers for the first time that it was Mordecai who had exposed the assassination plot, but nothing had been done to honour the great service he had done the king. As usual, he seems unable to act without advice, so he asks who is in the palace. He is told that Haman is there, hoping to speak to the king about having Mordecai hanged on the gallows he has prepared.

The scene that follows could come from a stage comedy (vv. 6 –11). The king asks Haman about ways of honouring someone. Haman assumes the king is talking about him, so says all the things he would like, such as royal robes, one of the king's horses, a royal crown—and a procession through the streets of the city. Excellent, the king agrees, then asks him to arrange all those things for the Jew Mordecai who sits at his gate. Haman, shocked and appalled, goes home 'mourning and with his head covered' (v. 12). Haman's wife Zeresh does nothing to cheer him up. 'If Mordecai... is of the Jewish people', she says, 'you will not prevail against him, but will surely fall before him' (v. 13).

Reflection

God moves in a mysterious way, his wonders to perform.

William Cowper, 1779

DAVID WINTER

Evil overthrown

So the king and Haman went in to feast with Queen Esther. On the second day, as they were drinking wine, the king again said to Esther, 'What is your petition, Queen Esther? It shall be granted you. And what is your request? Even to the half of my kingdom, it shall be fulfilled.' Then Queen Esther answered, 'If I have won your favour, O king, and if it pleases the king, let my life be given me— that is my petition—and the lives of my people—that is my request. For we have been sold, I and my people, to be destroyed, to be killed, and to be annihilated. If we had been sold merely as slaves, men and women, I would have held my peace; but no enemy can compensate for this damage to the king.' Then King Ahasuerus said to Queen Esther, 'Who is he, and where is he, who has presumed to do this?' Esther said, 'A foe and enemy, this wicked Haman!'

Before the events described above, Esther had done what she purposed and approached the king. He invited her into his presence warmly. Emboldened, she made a simple request. Could she give a banquet and invite Haman to it? Ahasuerus readily agreed—after all, at that point Haman was his most trusted courtier, bearing the royal signet ring (5:1–8).

Haman must have attended the banquet with some misgivings, but nothing would have prepared him for Esther's response to the king's invitation (which did not come until 'the second day' of feasting) to present a petition—anything, 'Even to the half of my kingdom' (v. 2). Esther did not want half the kingdom, just the lives of the one-time slaves of the empire, the Jews—including herself. She shrewdly suggested Haman's plan would create 'damage to the king' (v. 4). Ahasuerus, who had in fact agreed to Haman's proposal to deal with what he claimed was a potential threat to the unity of the kingdom, now professes ignorance: 'who has presumed to do this?' (v. 5). Esther's answer is concise and damning: 'A foe and enemy, this wicked Haman!' (v. 6).

Reflection

*Because Esther was prepared to 'perish', she was able to save
her people from perishing.*

DAVID WINTER

Come on and celebrate!

Haman son of Hammedatha the Agagite, the enemy of all the Jews, had plotted against the Jews to destroy them, and had cast Pur—that is, 'the lot'—to crush and destroy them; but when Esther came before the king, he gave orders in writing that the wicked plot that he had devised against the Jews should come upon his own head, and that he and his sons should be hanged on the gallows. Therefore these days are called Purim, from the word Pur. Thus... the Jews established and accepted as a custom for themselves and their descendants and all who joined them, that without fail they would continue to observe these two days every year, as it was written and at the time appointed.

Just in case readers might miss the subtleties of the plot, with all its twists and turns, we have here a very brief resumé of the story and a commandment that the two days Haman had chosen by lot ('Pur') on which to annihilate the Jews should be commemorated for ever. So, the Jewish feast of Purim came into being and is still celebrated. It is often very noisy, even slightly riotous!

Here we come to the end of the story of Esther and Mordecai as we have it in our Bibles. Its strangest feature, as we have seen, is the way in which divine providence—God's ordering of events to bring about his will—is ever-present in the story but never openly acknowledged. His hand is constantly active, but only visible to those who know what they are looking for.

Esther herself is a great Jewish heroine, thrust into a role she had not sought. She found herself the chief player in a tense battle of wits and courage, emerging as the human agent of her people's deliverance. Game, set and match to the Jews, we might say—or, more correctly, to the anonymous other who watched over them.

Reflection

Pause and give thanks for the ways in which God has providentially ordered your life, even though at the time you probably did not see it!

DAVID WINTER

63

Waiting for God's still, small voice

A request came through to the convent. The headteacher of the local high school wondered if the sisters would be willing to host a quiet day for some of the older pupils. Mother Superior laid down the letter and took a very deep breath. The local high school had a notorious reputation for unruliness and worse. She thought about her little community of sisters and how they spent most of their time in silence, work and prayer. How would they react to this invasion of their privacy and sanctity? To their credit, all the sisters agreed to the request, but, as the time drew closer, they began to brace themselves for the coming onslaught.

The day dawned bright and clear. The teenagers arrived and spread themselves out around the convent gardens—a breathtaking change from the downtown sink estates where most of them lived. The sun shone and the day passed remarkably peacefully. As they were leaving, the most senior boy, who was also one of the most infamous trouble-makers, came to Mother Superior to thank her, then added, 'May we please come again, Mother?' Before she could respond he went on, 'You see, until today I never knew what silence was. I had never heard a bird sing before today.' She hugged him and told him they would be welcome to come again, any time—and this time she meant it!

This true story tells us something about the power of contemplation. A contemplative heart is contagious. The teenagers picked up on the atmosphere of prayerful silence of their hostesses and shared it with each other. Contemplation can happen anywhere, in circumstances where we might not think it possible. A silenced heart hears things that we completely miss in our everyday busyness and noise.

When we share our own awareness of the gift of stillness of heart, as the sisters did, it is multiplied, not divided. Our true self begins to grow and flourish in a heart that has learned to be still, to attend to the holy, to listen for God's still, small voice and hear the birds sing.

As we journey through the next two weeks, we will explore something of what contemplative prayer might mean for us.

Margaret Silf

GENESIS 28:10–13, 16–17 (NRSV)

The Lord is in this place

Jacob left Beersheba and went towards Haran. He came to a
certain place and stayed there for the night, because the sun had
set. Taking one of the stones of the place, he put it under his head
and lay down in that place. And he dreamed that there was a ladder set up on the earth, the top of it reaching to heaven; and the
angels of God were ascending and descending on it. And the Lord
stood beside him and said, 'I am the Lord, the God of Abraham
your father and the God of Isaac...' Then Jacob woke from his
sleep and said, 'Surely the Lord is in this place—and I did not
know it!' And he was afraid, and said, 'How awesome is this place!
This is none other than the house of God, and this is the gate of
heaven.'

Whenever I hear the story of Jacob's ladder, I am reminded of a friend
who was diagnosed with a lingering and debilitating illness. As she was
trying to come to terms with the changed shape of her future, her husband of over 30 years decided that he could not cope with this and left
her to deal with it alone. We were reflecting together on this story when
she told me, very quietly: 'That's me. My life seems to have turned to
stone, but now I realise—the Lord is in this place and I never knew it!'

We do not expect our stony ground to become the place of revelation, yet this is precisely how it is for Jacob. We find ourselves in a situation of helplessness, where all we can do is sink down and bear it. We
cannot manufacture the ladder ourselves. We cannot make it happen. It
happens when we are at a place of inner stillness. In Jacob's case, this
was in deep, exhausted sleep.

Have you ever felt the touch of God's love upon your heart in the
midst of a situation where you felt bereft, lonely, frightened, helpless,
exhausted or at the end of your tether? That was the still, small voice.

Reflection
*When life gouges out deep hollows in our hearts, these can become the very
places that God will transform into pools of grace.*

MARGARET SILF

Turn aside

Moses was keeping the flock of his father-in-law Jethro, the priest of Midian; he led his flock beyond the wilderness, and came to Horeb, the mountain of God. There the angel of the Lord appeared to him in a flame of fire out of a bush; he looked, and the bush was blazing, yet it was not consumed. Then Moses said, 'I must turn aside and look at this great sight, and see why the bush is not burned up.' When the Lord saw that he had turned aside to see, God called to him out of the bush, 'Moses, Moses!' And he said, 'Come no closer! Remove the sandals from your feet, for the place on which you are standing is holy ground.' He said further, 'I am the God of your father, the God of Abraham, the God of Isaac, and the God of Jacob.' And Moses hid his face, for he was afraid to look at God.

The still point of revelation can happen when we are going about the very ordinary business of our lives: tending his father-in-law's flock was what Moses was doing, but for us it might be looking after our families and getting on with our daily work. The still, small voice is heard when we least expect it, but when it comes, it comes with life-changing power. Yet that power is always creative, never destructive. The bush burns, but is not consumed. That great power is always for the greater good, never solely for ourselves. God reminds Moses that the flow of grace has been given continually through all the generations. We are a part of the continuum.

This explosion of revelatory radiance in the burning bush evokes a response from Moses, who 'must turn aside to see' (v. 2). We will only hear the still, small voice when we too turn aside from our normal pre-occupations to attend to the holy in moments of quiet contemplative prayer. When God sees that we have turned aside, then the invitation is given: 'Come closer. Take off your sandals. You are standing on holy ground.'

Reflection

Take time to turn aside today and simply hold your heart open
for whatever God may be wanting to give you.

MARGARET SILF

Sending down roots

Blessed are those who trust in the Lord, whose trust is the Lord. They shall be like a tree planted by water, sending out its roots by the stream. It shall not fear when heat comes, and its leaves shall stay green; in the year of drought it is not anxious, and it does not cease to bear fruit.

Trees appear to do nothing. They are simply there, growing in the place where they are rooted and yet, in due season, they bear leaves, blossoms and fruit. All that is required of them, it seems, is to send down their roots to the ground water that gives them life. If that is in place there is nothing to fear. Even a season of drought cannot undermine the living presence they embody.

The trees give us a wonderful model of contemplative prayer. It is about sending down our roots to the depths of the ground water of our being, in God. We, however, find it hard to trust this divine wisdom. We are programmed, from our earliest years, to 'do', to achieve, to succeed. Of course the journey of faith also demands our effort, in living the gospel values in our daily lives. None of this will happen, though, if our roots are not immersed in the stream of God's love and grace.

To be attentive to the still, small voice, we need first and foremost to stay consciously connected to the source of our being, in stillness of heart and mind. If this is in place, all the rest will follow. If it is not, then there can be no leaves, no blossom, no enduring fruit on the tree we call our life.

God gives us God's own model of 'success' and 'achievement' in something as simple and beautiful as a tree. Look at a tree in the fullness of its blossom and you will see 'success'. Pluck the cherries and you will understand 'achievement'. All this happens because the trees send down their roots to the deep water.

Remember: in contemplative prayer we are doing nothing more than sending our roots deeper into the heart of God.

Reflection

*It is wisely said that God created us to be human beings,
not human doings.*

MARGARET SILF

Living water

A Samaritan woman came to draw water, and Jesus said to her, 'Give me a drink.' (His disciples had gone to the city to buy food.) The Samaritan woman said to him, 'How is it that you, a Jew, ask a drink of me, a woman of Samaria?'... Jesus answered her, 'If you knew the gift of God, and who it is that is saying to you, "Give me a drink," you would have asked him, and he would have given you living water.' The woman said to him, 'Sir, you have no bucket, and the well is deep. Where do you get that living water?... Jesus said to her, 'Everyone who drinks of this water will be thirsty again, but those who drink of the water that I will give them will never be thirsty. The water that I will give will become in them a spring of water gushing up to eternal life.' The woman said to him, 'Sir, give me this water, so that I may never be thirsty or have to keep coming here to draw water.'

Just as a tree puts down deep roots to reach for the nourishment and the water it needs for life, so we, too, must search for that life-giving water. The tree knows instinctively what to do. We, with our higher intellect, think that we know better how to arrive at what we need. We go to every kind of well in the hope of filling up our bucket, if only for one more day—material possessions, transient human relationships, superficial entertainment, shopping malls. We trudge again and again to these temporary wells and the thirst recedes for a short while, only to return more fiercely than before.

For the Samaritan woman, Jesus opens up a whole new vision of possibility: 'Bring your heart's longings to me,' he invites her, 'and you will find a source of love and joy and peace that will never fail you.'

She responds by sitting beside Jesus at the well and listening. Her only prayer now has become: 'Sir, give me this living water.'

Reflection

We open ourselves to the living water by sitting still and listening to the voice of God in our hearts.

MARGARET SILF

Distracted?

Now as they went on their way, he entered a certain village, where a woman named Martha welcomed him into her home. She had a sister named Mary, who sat at the Lord's feet and listened to what he was saying. But Martha was distracted by her many tasks; so she came to him and asked, 'Lord, do you not care that my sister has left me to do all the work by myself? Tell her then to help me.' But the Lord answered her, 'Martha, Martha, you are worried and distracted by many things; there is need of only one thing. Mary has chosen the better part, which will not be taken away from her.'

I always feel sorry for Martha and I am sure I am not alone in this. Recently I had the opportunity to stay with a small community of religious sisters in Canada, called the Marthas. I have rarely felt so wonderfully welcomed as I did in their home. On my first morning, they prepared a lovely breakfast for me and when I thanked them and expressed my surprise and delight at being invited so enticingly into the new day, they said simply, 'Margaret, you must understand, Marthas love to feed people.' What a calling! What a gift! I am sure Jesus also fully appreciated the Martha in his own life.

Perhaps the problem lies not so much in Martha's need and desire to prepare the meal, but in her distractedness. It is good, surely—indeed, very good—to serve each other, to minister to each other, to feed and care for each other. If, however, our outward service is not itself fed and nourished by quality time in stillness, attending to God's voice in our hearts, then it can easily become a distraction and a chore rather than true ministry. My Canadian Marthas, wonderful cooks though they were, were also, first and foremost, profoundly aware of their inner Mary.

There is a Martha and a Mary in each of us. Jesus welcomes them both, but challenges us to find a healthy balance between them and make sure that our Martha is being nourished by our Mary, and not the other way round.

Reflection
Have you fed your Mary today?

MARGARET SILF

Contemplation has consequences

[Jesus] entered Jericho and was passing through it. A man was there named Zacchaeus; he was a chief tax collector and was rich. He was trying to see who Jesus was, but on account of the crowd he could not, because he was short in stature. So he ran ahead and climbed a sycamore tree to see him, because he was going to pass that way. When Jesus came to the place, he looked up and said to him, 'Zacchaeus, hurry and come down; for I must stay at your house today.' So he hurried down and was happy to welcome him.

Zacchaeus is waiting, like us, for a glimpse of Jesus, for an echo of that still, small voice which reveals the presence of God.

I love to imagine this little man climbing a sycamore tree to get a better view. I guess he thought he would get one of the best seats that way, where he would also have the advantage of being out of sight and 'above the action', nice and safe on his treetop perch. That is certainly one way to 'wait', to catch a glimpse of glory without having to get involved in the consequences. Indeed, it is possible to engage in contemplative prayer in this way, spending quality time with God but without turning our contemplation into action.

Jesus, though, has other ideas. He must have been delighted that this notorious sinner—a tax-collector who exploited the ordinary people—wanted to see him so much that he climbed a sycamore tree for a better view. If ever there was a time to strike while the iron was hot, this was it. Jesus stops, right there beneath the sycamore tree, and has a still, small word with Zacchaeus. 'Come down. I am coming home with you today.' Zacchaeus comes down and responds to the call. The consequences of the encounter prove life-changing. He welcomes Jesus and he welcomes all that the meeting with Jesus will mean. Waiting for the still, small voice means being ready to enter into the consequences of what it has to say to us.

Reflection

Jesus is coming home to us today. Do we dare to come down from the tree?

MARGARET SILF

The sound of silence

[God said to Elijah] 'Go out and stand on the mountain before the Lord, for the Lord is about to pass by.' Now there was a great wind, so strong that it was splitting mountains and breaking rocks in pieces before the Lord, but the Lord was not in the wind; and after the wind an earthquake, but the Lord was not in the earthquake; and after the earthquake a fire, but the Lord was not in the fire; and after the fire a sound of sheer silence. When Elijah heard it, he wrapped his face in his mantle and went out and stood at the entrance of the cave. Then there came a voice to him, that said, 'What are you doing here, Elijah?'

In general it seems to be the case that the more words we need in order to say something, the less it is worth saying, and the bigger the clamour surrounding an issue, the less we are likely to hear the truth. Elijah was to discover this for himself, alone on the bare mountainside, struggling with plenty of issues of his own, yet engaging in this unlikely dialogue with the living God. He has a God-given intuition that he needs to be here in this desolate and exposed situation and it is precisely here he will sense the closeness of the divine mystery.

Then these other contenders for his attention arrive—the wind that splits his ears and his senses as well as the rocks, the earthquake that shakes the very basis of his imagined stability, the fire stripping away all that is not essential. Yet none of these experiences holds that elusive presence of God he is seeking. We, too, will not hear the precious word we long for in the relentless demands, the petrifying panics, the burning issues that can so easily dominate our lives.

After all of these comes sheer silence. Silence may frighten us more than all the clamour. In the silence there is no escape from ourselves. Yet, if we have the courage to wait, in faith, in that deep inner silence, we, too, will hear the still, small voice.

Reflection

May we seek today the silence beneath the noise.

MARGARET SILF

Waiting for sunrise

[Jesus said] 'Be dressed for action and have your lamps lit; be like those who are waiting for their master to return from the wedding banquet, so that they may open the door for him as soon as he comes and knocks. Blessed are those slaves whom the master finds alert when he comes; truly I tell you, he will fasten his belt and have them sit down to eat, and he will come and serve them. If he comes during the middle of the night, or near dawn, and finds them so, blessed are those slaves. But know this: if the owner of the house had known at what hour the thief was coming, he would not have let his house be broken into. You also must be ready, for the Son of Man is coming at an unexpected hour.'

An ancient fable tells of how a novice in the spiritual life once asked his master how he might reach communion with God. Instead of giving him an answer, the master asked a question in return. 'What can you do to make the sun rise?' The novice was disappointed, knowing of course that he could do absolutely nothing to make the sun rise. He became disheartened that all his attempts to pray appeared to be fruitless and totally ineffective. Eventually he went back to the master and asked him, perhaps a little petulantly, 'So why have you been teaching us all these methods and practices of prayer?'

The master answered him, 'To make sure that you are awake when the sun rises.'

Prayer is not about trying to change the mind of the unchanging God, but, rather, opening ourselves to the grace of being changed by the unchanging God. Like the novice in the story, we want results, but, in the passage, Jesus tells us that the secret lies in the waiting, not in any accomplishments of our own. We practise whichever forms of prayer help us to do this so that we, like the novice, will be ready and waiting, spiritually alert, when the master returns. That waiting is itself our prayer.

Reflection

Sunrise may surprise us at any moment. Let us be awake to rejoice in it.

MARGARET SILF

Soul growth

[Jesus] also said, 'The kingdom of God is as if someone would scatter seed on the ground, and would sleep and rise night and day, and the seed would sprout and grow, he does not know how. The earth produces of itself, first the stalk, then the head, then the full grain in the head. But when the grain is ripe, at once he goes in with his sickle, because the harvest has come.' He also said, 'With what can we compare the kingdom of God, or what parable will we use for it? It is like a mustard seed, which, when sown upon the ground, is the smallest of all the seeds on earth; yet when it is sown it grows up and becomes the greatest of all shrubs, and puts forth large branches, so that the birds of the air can make nests in its shade.'

Impatience is very much a characteristic of our times. We switch on the computer and expect to be immediately connected to our friends around the world. Any delay and we quickly complain about the technology. When we run short of bread or milk we go to the shop to get more. Most people today will never have baked bread or milked a cow. We have lost touch with the sense of a 'process'; we expect instant results.

It is hardly surprising that we sometimes see prayer in the same light. We ask God for what we think we want or need and feel let down if there are no obvious results. In today's reading, Jesus reminds us that our ways are not God's ways. God works silently, secretly, in the depths of our hearts, in ways that we are completely unaware of.

We do not sow seeds, then keep digging them up to see how they are doing. We trust the earth and sun and rain and the power in the seed itself to fulfil its destiny and become life-giving food. Can we trust God to bring to fruition the seed of the Spirit he has planted in our hearts, which he tends, day and night, without us being aware that he is doing it?

Reflection
Take the time to become who you truly are.

MARGARET SILF

Baby wisdom

O Lord, my heart is not lifted up, my eyes are not raised too high; I do not occupy myself with things too great and too marvellous for me. But I have calmed and quieted my soul, like a weaned child with its mother; my soul is like the weaned child that is with me. O Israel, hope in the Lord from this time on and for evermore.

A baby can teach us more about faith than a whole library of theology books. A baby believes that when you hold him, you will not let him fall. He believes that when he is hungry you will give him something to eat. He believes that when he is frightened you will hold and comfort him. He believes that when he is in pain or discomfort you will help him and attend to his needs.

A baby does not check your credentials or ask for certificates of competence. She has no idea whether you know anything about childcare or not. Above all, she does not worry about these things. Her entire relationship with you is based on trust alone. Babies do not just believe, they trust you.

I cherish a photo of my own daughter taken when she was a baby. She is lying in her pram, gazing at a fuchsia flower. The wonder in her eyes is palpable. She is gazing at the flower as if she were seeing the very first flower for the very first time. Such a sense of wonder is the gift of true contemplation. No wonder that Jesus calls us to 'become like children' (Matthew 18:3)—they have much to teach us.

It is this kind of trust that the psalmist is inviting us to discover—the trust of a small child who lies in her mother's arms without a worry in the world. Such trust is possible because the arms that hold us are the everlasting arms and the still place in which we are held, whether we realise it or not, is the place where, in calm and stillness, we will hear the still, small voice of our divine parent's love.

Reflection
May we learn to trust God as simply and completely as once we trusted the human arms that held us.

MARGARET SILF

Prayer without ceasing

Rejoice always, pray without ceasing, give thanks in all circumstances; for this is the will of God in Christ Jesus for you. Do not
quench the Spirit. Do not despise the words of prophets, but test
everything; hold fast to what is good; abstain from every form of
evil. May the God of peace himself sanctify you entirely; and may
your spirit and soul and body be kept sound and blameless at the
coming of our Lord Jesus Christ. The one who calls you is faithful,
and he will do this. Beloved, pray for us.

That would be some Lenten penance, you may be thinking—to 'pray
without ceasing'. Is it really a call to spend all our waking hours on our
knees in a cold, damp church? That might indeed quench the Spirit.
What could Paul possibly mean?

A birdwatcher friend helped me to understand this. He explained to
me how, from time to time, serious birdwatchers will spend time in a
hide, perhaps at a bird sanctuary, engaging in focused observation. They
will also be tuned in to the birdsong all around them, all the time. They
will know each bird's call, know who is arriving and who is migrating.
They will recognise the seasons for building nests, laying eggs, brood-
ing, hatching and raising the young. They will enter, lovingly and non-
intrusively, into the world of the birds, simply by attending to the
birdsong.

To pray without ceasing is to attend in this constant way to the subtle
movements of God within and around us. It is to become 'tuned in' to
all that God is saying—perhaps inviting us to rejoice in all that gives
life, perhaps warning us when we are going off course, perhaps alerting
us to the needs of others. When we stay 'tuned in' like this we can be
sure that the still, small voice will become audible.

From time to time we will also go into a 'hide' for more focused
contemplation, but contemplative awareness is not confined to being in
a hide—it can suffuse every moment of our lives.

Reflection

*Take time to notice the constant song of God's love running through your
life. What special notes have you been aware of today?*

MARGARET SILF

Closer than your own next breath

Surely, this commandment that I am commanding you today is not too hard for you, nor is it too far away. It is not in heaven, that you should say, 'Who will go up to heaven for us, and get it for us so that we may hear it and observe it?' Neither is it beyond the sea, that you should say, 'Who will cross to the other side of the sea for us, and get it for us so that we may hear it and observe it?' No, the word is very near to you; it is in your mouth and in your heart for you to observe.

A friend of mine ministered to people in a residential care home, most of whom suffered from advanced forms of dementia. At first the members of staff were sceptical about his plan to offer a time of quiet meditation each week for the residents, but he persisted and a number of the residents would come to these little gatherings. I was very moved by what he told me about how he led these people to the still place in their own hearts. He began by encouraging them to notice each breath they took, the breathing in and the breathing out. Then he invited them, with each breath, to breathe in the presence and love of God and breathe out their own concerns.

Then, most significantly, he suggested to them that whenever they felt lonely or lost, simply by becoming aware of each breath they took they would always know that they were never alone and God was with them constantly, closer to them than their own breathing. He told me how their faces lit up in little flashes of joy, to realise that God was with them at a place in their hearts deeper than all loneliness, closer than all their fears of feeling lost.

The still centre that we seek so earnestly is not beyond our reach in the heights of intellectual understanding or distant experiences of long-gone saints and mystics. It abides in our own hearts, closer to us than our own next breath.

Reflection

Contemplation is not an exercise of the mind so much as an affair of the heart.

MARGARET SILF

Streams in the desert

As a deer longs for flowing streams, so my soul longs for you, O God. My soul thirsts for God, for the living God. When shall I come and behold the face of God? My tears have been my food day and night, while people say to me continually, 'Where is your God?'... Deep calls to deep at the thunder of your cataracts; all your waves and your billows have gone over me. By day the Lord commands his steadfast love, and at night his song is with me, a prayer to the God of my life.

The women of Egypt provide the inspiration and focus for this year's Women's World Day of Prayer. More than most of us, the women—and the men and children—of Egypt have had reason in their recent history to cry out with all the passion of the psalmist as tears have been their food, night and day through the upheavals and sufferings of recent conflicts. More than most of us, they have had reason to call out of the depths of their heartache, 'Where is our God?'

Yet it is precisely those depths that take us to the heart of the matter. In the depths of our despair, far more than in our happier moments, we long for the living water, the living God. At the extremes of our experience, far more than when all is going smoothly, we go deeper into our hearts, longing for the groundwater that alone sustains us.

Today especially we join in solidarity with our sisters and brothers in Egypt, amid the roar of the cataracts of conflict and the storm clouds of suffering and loss, and ask God to speak that still, small word of peace at the core of our being, where 'deep calls to deep' (v. 7) and God's love is an ever-flowing stream in the deserts.

There is no depth of suffering to which we can sink where God is not already there, waiting to embrace us, deeper than the waves, more powerful than the cataracts, more eloquent than the thunder.

Reflection

When we go head to head with each other, there is conflict. When we meet heart to heart, there is peace and understanding.

MARGARET SILF

The rainfall of grace

For my thoughts are not your thoughts, nor are your ways my ways, says the Lord. For as the heavens are higher than the earth, so are my ways higher than your ways and my thoughts than your thoughts. For as the rain and the snow come down from heaven, and do not return there until they have watered the earth, making it bring forth and sprout, giving seed to the sower and bread to the eater, so shall my word be that goes out from my mouth; it shall not return to me empty, but it shall accomplish that which I purpose, and succeed in the thing for which I sent it.

A story is told of an old man in France who used to go every morning into his local church, where he would simply sit in the back row in silence and gaze into space. The parish priest noticed that this was happening and became concerned that perhaps the man was in need or difficulty of some kind. One day, when the man was just about to leave the church, the priest spoke to him, asking if he had any particular concern that was bringing him into church every morning.

The man assured the priest that he simply came to the church to pray and he described his prayer like this: 'I just gaze at him and he gazes at me.' There could hardly be a more complete or succinct description of contemplative prayer than this. We simply place ourselves consciously in the presence of God and allow him to gaze upon us with his infinite love.

Many would ask, 'What difference does it make?' 'Does it work?' Well, today's passage answers that question with a comparison that is as profoundly wise as it is beautiful. The rain and the snow have nothing to prove. They visit the earth, bring life and do not return to the heavens without fulfilling that purpose. So, too, our contemplative prayer opens our hearts to the rainfall of God's grace, which will never fail to fulfil its purpose in our hearts.

Reflection

May God's love penetrate our hearts as the sun, the rain and the snow penetrate the earth, bringing forth new life.

MARGARET SILF

Don't forget to renew your annual subscription to *New Daylight*! If you enjoy the notes, why not also consider giving a gift subscription to a friend or member of your family?

You will find subscription order forms on pages 156 and 157.
New Daylight is also available from your local Christian bookshop.

Bible stories rediscovered: Daniel

For those who went to Sunday school or equivalent in early childhood, there will be a few stories that stand out as being the most memorable and it is two of these that we shall be reading about during these next couple of weeks, both from the book of Daniel. The first is to do with a huge and terrifying fiery furnace into which three innocent men are thrown and miraculously survive. The second is to do with Daniel himself. Many children, even nowadays, will know that he was once thrown into a den of lions and, like his three friends in their furnace, he survived as the result of a miracle.

The book of Daniel is a book of two halves. There are six stories in the first half (chapters 1 to 6) and, in the second half (chapters 7 to 12), four visions given to Daniel. We read of Nebuchadnezzar, who was the powerful Babylonian king who first invaded Jerusalem in 605BC and removed from the city not only valuable furnishings from the temple but also captured some of the city's nobility. Among them were Daniel, Hananiah, Mishael and Azariah who were brought into the king's service (Daniel 1:1–6).

These four men become the heroes of the stories as they settle into life in the palace of this pagan king. Right from the start they show that they are not willing to compromise their faith in God. Despite the fact that the world as they knew it has collapsed around them and they find themselves in a most hostile environment far from home, they stay true to their conviction that though their city and temple may have collapsed, the God whom they worship is still all-powerful and sovereign, even in Babylon.

Not surprisingly, this conviction is greatly tested and, over the coming two weeks, we shall see how faith can not only survive but flourish when faced with a fiery furnace and den of lions. The stories of Daniel and his friends are much more than exciting tales of adventure—they are testimonies of genuine faith in action and how such faith has radical effects on the community.

Michael Mitton

Into captivity

> Then the king commanded his palace master Ashpenaz to bring some of the Israelites of the royal family and of the nobility, young men without physical defect and handsome, versed in every branch of wisdom, endowed with knowledge and insight, and competent to serve in the king's palace; they were to be taught the literature and language of the Chaldeans... Among them were Daniel, Hananiah, Mishael, and Azariah, from the tribe of Judah.

Our story begins at the time when Nebuchadnezzar defeated the combined forces of Egypt and Assyria at the battle of Carchemish, thereby becoming the most powerful king in the region. Although Judah was, comparatively, small-fry, he determined that it should come under his wing and not become a foothold for Egypt, should its forces recover and make a counter-attack. He clearly had a good look round the city while he was in Jerusalem and noticed that it had some assets worth taking back to Babylon, in particular some of the temple furnishings and a few of the city's royalty and leading civil servants. Thus, Daniel and his friends find themselves suddenly extracted from their homeland—princes and governors one day, and servants the next. The change must have been traumatic. Nebuchadnezzar's plan was to assimilate them into Babylonian life. He presumably imagined it would be fairly straightforward, but he failed to take account of two things: the strength of the men's faith and the power of their God.

Rather than behaving as victims, Daniel and his friends took immediate charge and, in the first chapter, we see them starting to make an impression. Nebuchadnezzar notices that they are men of unusual wisdom and insight (vv. 18–20). Daniel and his friends had decided that, though the environment was hostile, they could trust that God would be at work in it. There are times when we can feel very vulnerable, too, in an alien situation, where no one around us respects our faith. Daniel is a great example of one who saw such a situation not as a threat but as an opportunity.

Prayer
Lord, when my world feels hostile, grant me the faith Daniel had in you.

MICHAEL MITTON

Trouble begins

King Nebuchadnezzar made a golden statue whose height was sixty cubits and whose width was six cubits; he set it up on the plain of Dura in the province of Babylon. Then King Nebuchadnezzar sent for the satraps, the prefects, and the governors, the counsellors, the treasurers, the justices, the magistrates, and all the officials of the provinces to assemble and come to the dedication of the statue that King Nebuchadnezzar had set up.

Daniel's friends have been given the Babylonian names of Shadrach, Meshach and Abednego. Almost certainly these three names relate to Babylonian deities. Nebuchadnezzar no doubt hopes that, by giving them such names, he will bring them round to worshipping his gods. The king is the most powerful in the region, but even he is unable to change the hearts of the three men—as he discovers at the launch of his new super-statue, erected on the plain of Dura. According to Herodotus, Nebuchadnezzar built several of these massive statues, each the size of a ten-storey building, which in those days must have looked as if they reached the sky. The statue was erected as an object of worship and probably represented the god Nabu, after whom Nebuchadnezzar was named. We get the impression that size was important to this egocentric king, who also built a staged temple nearly 300 feet high in his city.

Nebuchadnezzar imagined that any sensible person would look on such grandeur and immensity and logically work out that the gods behind all this were worthy of worship—and the humans placed in charge by these gods worthy of admiration and devotion. None of this cuts any ice with Shadrach, Meshach and Abednego, however. Throughout history, we have seen leaders try to manipulate their people and enforce devotion by implementing all kinds of schemes, often using displays of power of one kind or another. Shadrach, Meshach and Abednego stand as people of real integrity who are not taken in by spin-doctors and advertisers, but instead keep true to the values of their faith.

Reflection

As you think about our world today, what are the equivalents of these statues of gold?

MICHAEL MITTON

Daniel 3:8–12 (NRSV)

The ultimate test

Accordingly, at this time certain Chaldeans came forward and denounced the Jews. They said to King Nebuchadnezzar, 'O king, live for ever! You, O king, have made a decree, that everyone who hears the sound of the horn, pipe, lyre, trigon, harp, drum, and entire musical ensemble, shall fall down and worship the golden statue, and whoever does not fall down and worship shall be thrown into a furnace of blazing fire. There are certain Jews whom you have appointed over the affairs of the province of Babylon: Shadrach, Meshach, and Abednego. These pay no heed to you, O King. They do not serve your gods and they do not worship the golden statue that you have set up.'

The king had made it clear: not to worship this statue meant a death sentence and a particularly cruel form of death at that. Shadrach and his friends can now be in no doubt about the stark truth: if they defy the king's command, they must face being plunged into the fiery furnace. You wonder what went through their minds as the horns, pipes and drums started up and the people all around them fell on their faces in devotion. What would go through our minds in such circumstances? Would courage rise or fall in our hearts? Through the ages, countless people of faith in places of fierce persecution have faced these terrifying choices and many, like Shadrach, Meshach and Abednego, have suffered cruel deaths because of their refusal to worship other gods.

For most of us, such brutal persecution is something that happens in far-off countries and is remote from our own experience, but stories like this do cause us to reflect on the depth of our faith. Should the ultimate test come, would we endure? Even if such questions are hypothetical, they serve to push us to explore just how deep our faith is. Have we developed a faith for the good times only or are we investing in all that makes for a faith so deep in our souls that losing it would be worse than losing our own lives?

Prayer

Pray for those who face active persecution and for the life of faith to run deep in your own heart.

MICHAEL MITTON

The inward conviction

> Shadrach, Meshach, and Abednego answered the king, 'O Nebuchadnezzar, we have no need to present a defence to you in this matter. If our God whom we serve is able to deliver us from the furnace of blazing fire and out of your hand, O king, let him deliver us. But if not, be it known to you, O king, that we will not serve your gods and we will not worship the golden statue that you have set up.'

Nebuchadnezzar is predictably furious with the three dissenters, but he clearly likes them for he offers them a second chance. He makes clear to them the consequences of their refusal to worship his gods—the fiery furnace—and he asks, 'Who is the god that will deliver you out of my hands?' (vv. 13–15). Shadrach, Meshach and Abednego remain defiant. For them, there is no question—the God they serve is more powerful than Nebuchadnezzar, his great statues and his blazing furnace.

This has now boiled down to a contest between the Babylonian gods, who look mighty powerful and impressive, and the Hebrew God, who has appeared less than powerful following the overthrowing of Jerusalem. Any impartial observer at the time may have looked at the events of recent years and concluded that he had fled his temple and his people, but this is not the way Shadrach and his friends see it. For them, Jerusalem and the temple may have gone, but their God remains more powerful than any idols humans might create.

These three men have come to a profound understanding: they believe God remains sovereign even when he does not perform acts of power and rescue, for they say, 'If our God… is able to deliver us'. They know there is a mystery about this God, but they are prepared to love and serve him to the end, even if he does not rescue them. Here we have three people who have become so devoted to God that their faith no longer depends on outward signs, but on inward conviction.

Prayer

Lord, even in those times when my eyes see no sign of your sovereign power, grant me the heart to know you are Lord of all.

MICHAEL MITTON

Into the fire

[Nebuchadnezzar] ordered some of the strongest guards in his army to bind Shadrach, Meshach, and Abednego and to throw them into the furnace of blazing fire. So the men were bound, still wearing their tunics, their trousers, their hats, and their other garments, and they were thrown into the furnace of blazing fire. Because the king's command was urgent and the furnace was so overheated, the raging flames killed the men who lifted Shadrach, Meshach, and Abednego. But the three men, Shadrach, Meshach, and Abednego, fell down, bound, into the furnace of blazing fire.

In the face of such defiance, Nebuchadnezzar is incandescent with rage. It is hard to know what enrages him more: the personal affrontery of these three men disobeying a direct royal command or their conviction that their God is more powerful than his. To make absolutely sure they are annihilated by the fire, he gets his men to stoke it up to full strength. Such fires were controlled by bellows, so it is supposed that seven bellows were used to establish maximum heat. The writer of this story goes into great detail, even describing their inflammable clothes, and such is the intensity of the fire that those ushering Shadrach and his friends into the furnace are killed.

We who know this story well know the outcome. Once known, the story takes on a different life. It is dramatic and exciting, but with a happy ending it carries no threat. Yet, if you were to hear this story for the first time, the moment you heard that the guards were instantly frizzled up by the fire, you would be forgiven for thinking that this would be the sad conclusion. The tale would be about courageous heroes who braved much for the sake of their convictions. Just occasionally in life, however, an astonishing rescue happens, and it only has to happen once for us to know it can happen any time. A story like this, if nothing else, tells us that even an apparently tragic tale can have a bright outcome.

Reflection
Can you think of stories in your life when you expected things to work out badly, but God wrote a different ending?

MICHAEL MITTON

The fourth man

Then King Nebuchadnezzar was astonished and rose up quickly. He said to his counsellors, 'Was it not three men that we threw bound into the fire?' They answered the king, 'True, O king.' He replied, 'But I see four men unbound, walking in the middle of the fire, and they are not hurt; and the fourth has the appearance of a god.' Nebuchadnezzar then approached the door of the furnace of blazing fire and said, 'Shadrach, Meshach, and Abednego, servants of the Most High God, come out! Come here!' So Shadrach, Meshach, and Abednego came out from the fire.

The king is able to see what is going on inside the furnace and he can tell that the three men have not been consumed by the fire. As if this is not miraculous enough, there is another cause for astonishment: there are now four people in the furnace, all walking around as if they are meeting for an afternoon cup of tea! As Nebuchadnezzar looks at this fourth man, he notes that he has the appearance of a god. There can be no doubt that the fourth 'man' in the furnace is an angel of God, sent to protect the three faithful friends (v. 28). The amazed king calls the men out and the writer, again with an eye for detail, tells us that the men's hair and robes were not singed and they do not even smell smoky (v. 27). The protection has been total.

The revealing part of the story is the way Nebuchadnezzar addresses the three men as 'servants of the Most High God'. This was not a contest between a king and rebellious subjects; it was a trial of the gods. Nebuchadnezzar comes away from it declaring that Shadrach and his friends serve a God who must be considered the 'Most High God'.

Our God is one who will not be conformed to the rational ways of this world, but from time to time displays his power in wonderful and miraculous ways. He may choose to perform his signs and wonders through any of us.

Prayer

*Lord, perform your wonders in our day that all may see
your great love and strength.*

Michael Mitton

The faith of the unbeliever

Nebuchadnezzar said, 'Blessed be the God of Shadrach, Meshach, and Abednego, who has sent his angel and delivered his servants who trusted in him. They disobeyed the king's command and yielded up their bodies rather than serve and worship any god except their own God. Therefore I make a decree: any people, nation, or language that utters blasphemy against the God of Shadrach, Meshach, and Abednego shall be torn limb from limb, and their houses laid in ruins; for there is no other god who is able to deliver in this way.'

The turnaround in Nebuchadnezzar is truly remarkable. One moment he is hurling the three men into his superheated furnace and the next he is extolling the God whom they so determinedly serve. Chapter 4 goes on to show how his faith in God remains deep in him. Nebuchadnezzar believes in the Lord following the display of his power.

We might think that such displays would always lead to a dramatic change of heart, but there are other stories in the Bible where this does not happen. The most notable is in 1 Kings 18:1—19:2 where, following the extraordinary display of power by the Lord through Elijah on Mount Carmel, Jezebel shows no intention of departing from her beliefs. Nebuchadnezzar is a powerful pagan king, but, in the stories from these chapters in Daniel, it is clear that he has an open mind. The bitter hearts of Jezebel and Ahab caused them to fail to grasp or even see God's great works.

Sometimes, those outside our faith community have a greater capacity to see the signs and wonders of God than those who should know better. Those of us who are established members of churches can settle into a reduced view of God and his ways, whereas those from outside can actually be quicker to see signs of God at work. They do, however, need the likes of Shadrach, Meshach and Abednego to introduce them to this God whose hand they glimpse in the workings of the world.

Reflection

Think about the friends you have who may be catching glimpses of God's power in action in their lives. Can you find opportunities to speak with them?

MICHAEL MITTON

Daniel: a listener in the depths

Daniel said: 'Blessed be the name of God from age to age, for wisdom and power are his. He changes times and seasons, deposes kings and sets up kings; he gives wisdom to the wise and knowledge to those who have understanding. He reveals deep and hidden things; he knows what is in the darkness, and light dwells with him. To you, O God of my ancestors, I give thanks and praise, for you have given me wisdom and power, and have now revealed to me what we asked of you, for you have revealed to us what the king ordered.'

We now move on to a story about Daniel. With his three friends from the fiery furnace, he made a great impression on King Nebuchadnezzar who, on matters of wisdom, has found the four of them 'ten times better' than any of his magicians (1:20). When the king had a troubling dream, he would consult his assortment of magicians and astrologers and challenge them not only to interpret his dream but even to know what it was without his telling them. Not surprisingly, they found it a tricky assignment!

Daniel, however, is up to the task and tells the king that no human can explain this dream; only God can (2:27–28). As Daniel is one who has deeply listened to God, he has heard from him about the dream and its meaning. Nebuchadnezzar is delighted and concludes, 'Truly, your God is God of gods' (v. 47). His confidence in Daniel is so strong that he places him in a position of high authority (v. 48).

In the midst of this dream story come the words in today's passage. This beautiful song of praise reveals the depth of Daniel's faith. He may be in a potentially dangerous and hostile place, but, as he turns his eyes to heaven, he sees the God who rules over all earthly things. Moreover, he is a God who knows what is in the darkness. For Daniel, there is no darkness where the light of God cannot shine.

Reflection

Spend time in focused attention on the God who is more powerful than the powers of this world and whose light will shine in any darkness.

MICHAEL MITTON

Trap-setting satraps

Soon Daniel distinguished himself above all the other presidents and satraps because an excellent spirit was in him, and the king planned to appoint him over the whole kingdom. So the presidents and the satraps tried to find grounds for complaint against Daniel in connection with the kingdom. But they could find no grounds for complaint or any corruption, because he was faithful, and no negligence or corruption could be found in him.

The Babylonian empire was short-lived. When Nebuchadnezzar died, 25 years after the fall of Jerusalem, it started to collapse. Within seven years, the throne had changed hands three times. At this point, Cyrus the Persian was the rising star. He had conquered the huge Median Empire and overran Babylon easily in 539BC. At the beginning of Daniel 6 we are told that Darius is in charge of Babylon. There is no record of Darius outside of the Bible, but it is clear that he is the one appointed by Cyrus to govern Babylon. He did this by appointing 120 satraps, and over them were three vice-regents, one of whom was Daniel. So impressed was Darius with Daniel's work that he planned to set him over the whole kingdom (6:3).

It was perhaps inevitable that this should lead to jealousy in the vice-regents and satraps and, indeed, they make plans to have him removed. They can find no charge to bring against him, but devise another cunning plan. They persuade Darius to issue an edict that, for the next 30 days, people may pray only to him or else be thrown to the lions. Presumably vanity gets the better of Darius, for he agrees. The satraps know that Daniel will only pray to his God, so they think they have got him.

Although, for many of us, mockery and persecution for our faith are mild compared to what some Christians have to face, there are times when we meet with hostility because of what we believe. Daniel is a wonderful example of someone who stands firm and refuses to compromise. He neither becomes defensive nor fearful, but trusts God.

Prayer

Lord, when I meet with hostility because of my faith and beliefs, grant me Daniel's deep-seated trust.

MICHAEL MITTON

A room with a view

Although Daniel knew that the document had been signed, he continued to go to his house, which had windows in its upper room open towards Jerusalem, and to get down on his knees three times a day to pray to his God and praise him, just as he had done previously. The conspirators came and found Daniel praying and seeking mercy before his God.

Daniel's response to the news of the conspiracy against him is typical: he is quite unwilling to compromise his faith, so he goes to his house and says his prayers. He knows that he is deliberately flouting the new decree that is written in stone and from which no exceptions can be made. As he climbs the stairs to the upper room and prepares to kneel down, he knows that, barring an intervention from God, he is signing his own death warrant—one that will be carried out by the teeth of hungry lions. Though many miles from his beloved homeland, he knows its direction and, facing it, he gazes out of the window, proclaiming praises to his God.

From outside the window, Daniel may have heard the footsteps of the satraps coming to catch him in his act of rebellion. Maybe some of us, had we been there, would have beseeched Daniel to soften his voice, step back from the window and find more subtle ways of saying his prayers, but this was not Daniel's way. In his mind's eye he could see Jerusalem and the holy temple, not in ruins but filled with the glory of God. He saw not a group of conniving hostile men, but a God who was committed to protecting his people. He saw nothing to make him afraid and everything to make him hope and rejoice.

When we face tough situations in life, we need to remember Daniel and pray for his eyesight—that we may see not with the eyes of fear and failure but those of faith and hope. Such eyesight develops when we worship God.

Reflection

How can you train the eyes of your heart to see beyond the things that cause you to fear?

MICHAEL MITTON

The law of the Medes and the Persians

When the king heard the charge, he was very much distressed. He was determined to save Daniel, and until the sun went down he made every effort to rescue him. Then the conspirators came to the king and said to him, 'Know, O king, that it is a law of the Medes and Persians that no interdict or ordinance that the king establishes can be changed.' Then the king gave the command, and Daniel was brought and thrown into the den of lions. The king said to Daniel, 'May your God, whom you faithfully serve, deliver you!'

The writer of this story makes it clear that the king should carry no blame in this tale. The conspirators are the ones who are at fault and have tricked the king into sentencing Daniel to death. There is also another power at work, however, a greater power than the king's, which is the 'law of the Medes and Persians' (v. 15).

The massive empire of Cyrus, which stretched from today's Turkey to the borders of India, was governed by unshakeable laws. Powerful though he is, the king has no power to change these laws and, despite his personal distress, he has to summon his guards to take Daniel to the opening of the pit of lions and throw him in. As Daniel is dragged towards this fearsome pit, he sees the forlorn look in the king's eyes and knows that not even a mighty king can rescue him.

We are clearly meant to understand at this point in the story that Daniel stands as a righteous man facing the most powerful opposition imaginable. The writer wants to make it clear that no human could be more vulnerable at this moment: conspirators, empires and raging lions are the threats he has to face. Yet, as we read this beautifully told tale, there is a sense that Daniel is as calm as Christ before Pilate, utterly at peace and paradoxically in control of the whole story. No human powers are a match for the power of God at work in faithful people.

Prayer

*Lord, when the powers of this world threaten to overwhelm me,
grant me the serenity of Daniel.*

MICHAEL MITTON

Another angle... Another angel

Then, at break of day, the king got up and hurried to the den of lions. When he came near the den where Daniel was, he cried out anxiously to Daniel, 'O Daniel, servant of the living God, has your God whom you faithfully serve been able to deliver you from the lions?' Daniel then said to the king, 'O king, live for ever! My God sent his angel and shut the lions' mouths so that they would not hurt me, because I was found blameless before him; and also before you, O king, I have done no wrong.'

We are not told why there was a den of lions in the king's palace, but clearly one of its purposes was capital punishment (6:7). Daniel is lowered into the pit and the entrance is sealed. As far as the king is concerned, this manner of execution provides one slender thread of hope. It is just possible that Daniel's God will have power over the lions and they will decide that Daniel is not a tasty meal. The king spends the night fasting and hoping and, at first light, dashes to the pit. Although paradoxically he is the one who sentenced Daniel to death, it is he who longs for him to live.

The sound of Daniel's voice coming from the den must have been both delightful and awesome. Daniel has been vindicated. He knew he had done no wrong and had nothing to fear. As he was lowered into that dark growling pit, he sensed another presence—an angel sent at the bidding of the God more powerful than any Mede, Persian or wild beast. As with the three in the fiery furnace, a holy presence gives protection from the destructive forces of this world.

This is the last of the six great stories in Daniel before the visions of the following chapters. The message in each of them is about the power and authority of God in a world where many refuse to acknowledge his presence, but where those with the eyes to see (like Darius) can find him.

Reflection
Can you think of time in your experience when you saw God's power and authority at work?

MICHAEL MITTON

A kingdom that cannot be destroyed

[Darius wrote] 'I make a decree, that in all my royal dominion people should tremble and fear before the God of Daniel: for he is the living God, enduring for ever. His kingdom shall never be destroyed, and his dominion has no end. He delivers and rescues, he works signs and wonders in heaven and on earth; for he has saved Daniel from the power of the lions.' So this Daniel prospered during the reign of Darius and the reign of Cyrus the Persian.

It would have been interesting to have seen the expressions on the faces of the conspirators when a radiant Daniel was hoisted up from the pit without so much as a claw mark on him. Their fate is to be thrown into the pit themselves with their families. The lions, now untethered by any angel, devour them. This detail is included, no doubt, to make clear that these were real lions with real appetites and it was a true miracle that Daniel was not killed. God had intervened with angelic protection and against such protection no hungry lion could prevail.

We have seen that Darius is already impressed by Daniel, but now his response shows how impressed he is by Daniel's God. He issues a decree that from now on, everyone throughout his dominion should reverence this God. He has clearly gained some insight into Daniel's God—that he is a God whose kingdom is different from the faltering kingdoms of this world, which all too easily come and go. This God has an eternal kingdom. This God is one who does extraordinary and remarkable things, rescuing people in hopeless situations and visiting them with signs and wonders.

It is interesting that it is Darius, a pagan, who gets a wonderful glimpse of the kingdom of God that is so full of miracles. He has watched Daniel carefully and his faith has made a deep impression on him. There are many today, too, who are open to 'getting the message' when they see God's people living lives that demonstrate how he is alive, loving, powerful and active here and now.

Prayer

Father, give me an open heart to your wonders, that I and others
with open eyes may glimpse heaven.

MICHAEL MITTON

Stories with a timeless message

When that period was over, I, Nebuchadnezzar, lifted my eyes to heaven, and my reason returned to me. I blessed the Most High, and praised and honoured the one who lives for ever. For his sovereignty is an everlasting sovereignty, and his kingdom endures from generation to generation. All the inhabitants of the earth are accounted as nothing, and he does what he wills with the host of heaven and the inhabitants of the earth.

For our final reading, we return to Nebuchadnezzar and his song of praise to the God he discovered through the witness of Daniel, Shadrach, Meshach and Abednego. This pagan king has seen the life of God in the exiles from Jerusalem and here declares God's sovereignty over heaven and earth. Many biblical scholars believe that these stories were gathered together and became especially significant at another time of suffering. The Seleucid King Antiochus Epiphanes began a terrible persecution of the Jewish people in the mid-160s BC, introducing the cult of Zeus into the temple. It was a violent and terrifying time for God's people in Jerusalem, but, during those years of terror, they went to the book of Daniel for the stories of faith that we have been revisiting over the past two weeks. In these stories they found hope that even the likes of Nebuchadnezzar and Darius could change their ways. They discovered how God could use the faithful witness of his people, even when everything around seemed to speak of chaos and destruction. The truth of the matter was that God was in ultimate control of the world.

The stories of the fiery furnace and the lions' den are not there just to entertain children. They are stories of rugged faith that have heartened God's people in times of trial and suffering and led them into visions of hope and faith. They do not solve the problem of suffering—many faithful people have died from flames and wild beasts—but they do draw us into a greater vision of the kingdom of God and his authority in this world.

Reflection

What has God been saying to you personally through these readings from Daniel?

MICHAEL MITTON

The faith of John Donne

The notes for the next two weeks are about John Donne, the poet and priest who lived at about the same time as Shakespeare. This time of year includes the anniversary of his death in 1631 (31 March), when the Anglican Church commemorates him. Some might wonder why a poet, some of whose writings are, to put it mildly, raunchy, has ended up in the official calendar alongside 'real' saints like the apostles, Benedict and Francis of Assisi. It is because he is designated as a 'spiritual writer', alongside theological and devotional authors, and his work (as well as his life) has important things to say about how we can be Christians now.

In two weeks, I can only scratch the surface and, inevitably, will have to miss out some favourites, but this is the man who gave us, 'Go, and catch a falling star' and 'A bracelet of bright hair about the bone', so even these few glances offer great riches. Donne burrows into our innermost feelings and fears; he strips away the comforting pretences of polite religion and leads us naked before God. Read him and the hairs on the back of your neck stand on end; you are carried away to the throne of grace. He does not just try to scare us, but is winkling out what really matters.

His life seems strikingly modern, as he was scratching around for a job and a place to live for many years, after secretly marrying his boss's niece. He lost his employment, his home and his position in society and was even thrown into prison by his father-in-law for a while. It was many years before he regained some kind of security. Perhaps he could be the patron saint of the unemployed.

The ruin of these worldly ambitions came after he had abandoned—some would say betrayed—the faith of his family. The Donnes were ardent Catholics: his uncle was martyred for his beliefs, and his brother died in jail, having been imprisoned for helping a Catholic priest. He left this behind, first to become a soldier and courtier, then later, even more so, to become a Church of England priest. By the end of his life, he was Dean of St Paul's Cathedral, often preaching before the king and part of the establishment. Amazingly, his monument in the Cathedral was the only one to survive the Great Fire of London in 1666.

When you mix all this with the death of several of his children and his own illnesses—when he himself seemed likely to die—his was a life of extremes. He has much to teach us.

Rachel Boulding

I am involved in mankind

Therefore, since we are justified by faith, we have peace with God through our Lord Jesus Christ, through whom we have obtained access to this grace in which we stand; and we boast in our hope of sharing the glory of God. And not only that, but we also boast in our sufferings, knowing that suffering produces endurance, and endurance produces character, and character produces hope, and hope does not disappoint us, because God's love has been poured into our hearts through the Holy Spirit that has been given to us.

This is a good place to start a fortnight with John Donne—a reading about being justified and obtaining access to grace, but also about suffering. Donne knew plenty about this. He offers his writing, preaching and whole life to God and links his own griefs, such as those in his many bereavements and illnesses, to those of Jesus.

The search for wholeness extends throughout Donne's life, as he strives to bring together his personal passions—encompassing physical love, strong friendship and his desire for God—with his enquiring mind. He had a sharp sense of inner conflict, but also a profound integrity, a unified take on thinking and feeling. As T.S. Eliot noted, when contrasting him with later poets, they did 'not feel their thought as immediately as the odour of a rose. A thought to Donne was an experience; it modified his sensibility.'

This extended beyond himself, outwards, because, as he put it in what has become one of the most celebrated expressions of our shared humanity in world literature, 'No man is an island, entire of itself; every man is a piece of the continent, a part of the main; if a clod be washed away by the sea, Europe is the less, as well as if a promontory were, as well as if a manor of thy friend's or of thine own were; any man's death diminishes me, because I am involved in mankind, and therefore never send to know for whom the bell tolls; it tolls for thee' ('Meditation XVII', 1624).

Prayer

Father, help me to realise the ways in which we all belong together, sharing and revelling in your love. Amen

RACHEL BOULDING

LUKE 1:28–31 (KJV, ABRIDGED)

Engaging brain as well as heart

And the angel came in unto [Mary], and said, Hail, thou that art highly favoured... And when she saw him, she was troubled at his saying, and cast in her mind what manner of salutation this should be. And the angel said unto her, Fear not, Mary: for thou hast found favour with God. And, behold, thou shalt conceive in thy womb, and bring forth a son, and shalt call his name Jesus.

Tomorrow is the feast of the Annunciation, celebrating Gabriel's announcement to Mary that she is to have a child, so I would like to look at 'Annunciation', the second in a series of seven poems (known as the 'La Corona' series), where the last line of each becomes the first line of the next one. One aspect of Donne's sense of integrity that we saw yesterday is the way that his imagination is drawn to intellectual puzzles and ironies. He delights in the idea of God planning the incarnation of his son before the beginning of time, on a cosmic scale. Addressing Mary (she is the 'thou' here), Donne teases out the notion of the creature, Mary, becoming the mother of her creator:

Ere by the spheres time was created, thou
Wast in his mind, who is thy Son, and Brother;
Whom thou conceivest, conceived; yea, thou art now
Thy Maker's maker, and thy Father's mother...

This is mind-boggling, its ideas spiralling out into the depths of the universe. It speaks of a bright, sparky faith that revels in paradox. Perhaps it could remind us that Christianity encompasses the brain as well as the emotions. We are to love the Lord our God with all our heart and mind and soul and strength. Donne does not divide these up. The end of the poem, running straight on from the lines above, thrills the heart as well as the mind:

Thou hast light in dark, and shutt'st in little room
Immensity, cloister'd in thy dear womb.

Prayer
Father, kindle in my mind, as well as my heart, the fire of your love.

RACHEL BOULDING

See with faith's eye

Then said Mary unto the angel, How shall this be, seeing I know not a man? And the angel answered and said unto her, The Holy Ghost shall come upon thee… For with God nothing shall be impossible. And Mary said, Behold the handmaid of the Lord; be it unto me according to thy word.

Today, the Annunciation, we look forward to the incarnation, to Christmas itself, exactly nine months away. In 'Nativity', the third poem of the 'La Corona' series, Donne pushes the paradoxes we have looked at so far still further, but, crucially, develops his line of thought beyond the ironies of yesterday—of Mary being her 'Maker's maker'. Here he looks at Jesus' humility in coming to save us and, more importantly, moves towards what his own response could be:

See'st thou, my soul, with thy faith's eyes, how He
Which fills all place, yet none holds Him, doth lie?
Was not His pity towards thee wondrous high,
That would have need to be pitied by thee?

Donne considers how wondrous it is that the cosmic God, who cannot be contained in any single place, should love and pity humankind so much that he comes to earth and makes himself subject to our own love and pity. He becomes vulnerable—liable to be hurt by people like us—offering himself as a fragile human baby, in an approach that we can easily reject. It is so simple to wound him. We have all done so, often by our casual ways of ignoring him and living as if he did not matter to our lives—when he is the one who gave us that life in the first place! In this poem, Donne encourages us to respond with our imagination, following Jesus in our hearts, and with a sense of the suffering that we share with Mary. He tells his soul:

Kiss him, and with him into Egypt go,
With his kind mother, who partakes thy woe.

Prayer

Lord Jesus Christ, you have offered yourself in love for me. Draw me nearer to you, that my feeble love can reflect yours.

RACHEL BOULDING

Facing my 'sin of fear'

'Abraham believed God, and it was reckoned to him as righteousness.' Now to one who works, wages are not reckoned as a gift but
as something due. But to one who without works trusts him who
justifies the ungodly, such faith is reckoned as righteousness.

Now we are back in Lent and can follow where John Donne leads during
this season, when the church encourages us to think about our sins. This
can be a positive exercise, involving clear-eyed examination of our fail-
ings. This is where Donne has much to tell us, with his talent for bur-
rowing into our most twisted motivations and fears. In 'A Hymn to God
the Father', Donne probes the depths of his own sinfulness, asking God:

Wilt Thou forgive that sin, through which I run,
And do run still, though still I do deplore?
When Thou hast done, Thou hast not done,
For I have more...

He makes puns using his own name ('done' being how 'Donne' is pronounced) and that of his wife, Anne More. He wants God to have him,
but, instead, is possessed by fears that his continuing sins have put too
much distance between him and God. He longs to sense God's presence (when God 'shall shine') as he has experienced it, but is terrified
that he will fail to do so when he dies, so continues:

I have a sin of fear, that when I have spun
   My last thread, I shall perish on the shore;
      But swear by Thyself, that at my death Thy Son
Shall shine as he shines now, and heretofore;
      And having done that, Thou hast done;
I fear no more.

Donne achieves a fragile resolution by urging God the Father to swear
that Jesus 'shall shine' at Donne's death. His fears will be allayed only
if this happens and, perhaps, he does not sound certain that it will.

Prayer
Father, help me to sense your love, despite my fears. Amen

RACHEL BOULDING

Batter my heart

So also David speaks of the blessedness of those to whom God reckons righteousness irrespective of works: 'Blessed are those whose iniquities are forgiven, and whose sins are covered; blessed is the one against whom the Lord will not reckon sin.'

These verses from Romans run straight on from the ones we read yesterday. There, Donne portrayed his 'sin of fear' as the sin of despair—of doubting that God's goodness is enough to save him. This is the sin dramatised in plays such as *Dr Faustus* (by Christopher Marlowe, staged when Donne was a young man) and *Damned by Despair*, written a couple of years after this poem, in the 1620s, by a Spanish Friar, Tirso de Molina. In both these plays, salvation is offered to a character who has a chance to respond to God's love but finds it impossible to believe.

This can be baffling to a modern audience, as most people misunderstand religion as involving being good. If you are nice, you will go to heaven. Actually, however, we are saved by grace—God's gift—which does not depend on our actions. The people in the plays, like Donne's depiction of himself, struggle to credit how God could possibly want them. They have committed lurid sins of sex and violence, but Donne's evocation of this temptation brings it closer to home. Like most of us, at some point, he finds it hard to believe that God could really love us. He wants to believe, but wants God to demonstrate his love to be sure.

Donne's way of countering these fears is to beg God to sweep him up and convince him thoroughly. He wants to be beaten into submission, in a way that verges on the unhealthy:

Batter my heart, three-person'd God; for you
As yet but knock; breathe, shine, and seek to mend;
That I may rise, and stand, o'erthrow me, and bend
Your force, to break, blow, burn, and make me new…
Take me to you, imprison me, for I,
Except you enthrall me, never shall be free,
Nor ever chaste, except you ravish me. (Holy Sonnet XIV)

Reflection
When I lack Donne's passion for God, what am I missing out on?

RACHEL BOULDING

Death, whom thy death slew

But now is Christ risen from the dead, and become the firstfruits of them that slept. For since by man came death, by man came also the resurrection of the dead. For as in Adam all die, even so in Christ shall all be made alive… For he must reign, till he hath put all enemies under his feet. The last enemy that shall be destroyed is death.

This passage leads us on from Donne's passionate approach to life to one of his most important themes, that of death. In a later poem in the 'La Corona' sequence, 'Resurrection', he revels in the paradoxes of the death of death:

Moist with one drop of Thy blood, my dry soul
Shall—though she now be in extreme degree
Too stony hard, and yet too fleshly—be
Freed by that drop, from being starved, hard or foul,
And life by this death abled shall control
Death, whom Thy death slew…

This recalls the tantalising ending of *Dr Faustus* (see yesterday's notes), where Faustus has only to reach out to Christ to be saved, but, in a gut-wrenching scene, cannot bring himself to do so.

Donne, in the words of T.S. Eliot, knew 'the ague of the skeleton'. It was not just that he lived in an age of uncertain mortality (a number of his children died young, as well as his beloved wife); more than this, he was preoccupied with death. On more than one occasion, through serious illness, he faced his own imminent end. For those of us who have had some sense of this (I have had an inkling of it myself, having had breast cancer), it can feel strange to move from death as something that happens to other people to its happening to yourself, possibly quite soon.

Of course we all have to die, yet we can be absolutely certain of God's strong love for each of us. He has created each one of us and loves us dearly. Jesus has destroyed death. It still has the power to hurt, but its ultimate sway has been comprehensively annihilated.

Reflection
Dare you trust God's love enough to think about your own death?

RACHEL BOULDING

1 CORINTHIANS 15:54–57 (KJV)

Death, be not proud

So when this corruptible shall have put on incorruption, and this mortal shall have put on immortality, then shall be brought to pass the saying that is written, Death is swallowed up in victory. O death, where is thy sting? O grave, where is thy victory? The sting of death is sin; and the strength of sin is the law. But thanks be to God, which giveth us the victory through our Lord Jesus Christ.

Donne wrote many of his 'Holy Sonnets' while relying on others for money and accommodation, and unsuccessfully applying for jobs. Yet these are among his most celebrated works.

Death, be not proud, though some have called thee
Mighty and dreadful, for thou art not so;
For those, whom thou think'st thou dost overthrow,
Die not, poor Death, nor yet canst thou kill me…
Thou art slave to Fate, chance, kings, and desperate men,
And dost with poison, war, and sickness dwell,
And poppy, or charms can make us sleep as well,
And better than thy stroke; why swell'st thou then?
One short sleep past, we wake eternally,
And death shall be no more; Death, thou shalt die. (Holy Sonnet X)

This seems like a great blast in the face of death—'Get lost, I am not afraid!'—but even here I think there is a sense that Donne does not quite believe his own rhetoric; the bravado leaves behind it the merest hint of doubt. As with his 'sin of fear' in the poem we read two days ago, Donne seems to be desperately trying to convince himself. The demise of death is still in the future: it 'shall be no more' at some point, but, at the moment, it is still causing us searing, unbearable pain.

If this were not the case, we might all be dancing at funerals. Even though we believe that our loved ones are with God, in that greater light, it is still a bitter wrench and we are weighed down by grief.

Prayer

Father, draw me towards the truth of your eternal life in the face of the losses in this life.

RACHEL BOULDING

I shall be made Thy music

Blessed be the God and Father of our Lord Jesus Christ, the Father of mercies and the God of all consolation, who consoles us in all our affliction, so that we may be able to console those who are in any affliction with the consolation with which we ourselves are consoled by God. For just as the sufferings of Christ are abundant for us, so also our consolation is abundant through Christ.

This passage follows on well from yesterday's reading about death, as Donne sought consolation in the face of the deaths he mourned, especially those of his wife and children. So here are some lines from 'Hymn to God my God, in my Sickness', written some years after yesterday's poem, when Donne was seriously ill with a fever from which many others died. He knew that he might not survive, but also that he might soon join in with the praise in heaven:

Since I am coming to that holy room,
Where, with Thy choir of saints for evermore,
I shall be made Thy music...

He reflects on his sins and his hopes of being saved by Christ:

So, in His purple wrapped, receive me, Lord;
By these His thorns, give me His other crown;
And as to others' souls I preached Thy word,
Be this my text, my sermon to mine own,
Therefore that He may raise, the Lord throws down.

Now that his hopes for heaven are not for some vague time in the future, he enters a heart-wringing plea ('give me...')—as he is being thrown down by disease. The last line reflects Job 22:29: 'When men are cast down, then thou shalt say, There is lifting up' (KJV).

This is surely a prayer that we would want to say, in some form, in times of crisis when we are 'thrown down', and also on our deathbed. Other things are stripped away and there is only God and us.

Reflection

How do you pray when you are thrown down?

RACHEL BOULDING

Reaching hard knowledge

And now, O Lord my God, thou hast made thy servant king instead
of David my father: and I am but a little child: I know not how to
go out or come in... Give therefore thy servant an understanding
heart to judge thy people, that I may discern between good and
bad: for who is able to judge this thy so great a people? And the
speech pleased the Lord, that Solomon had asked this thing.

Today is the anniversary of Donne's death, 383 years ago. One way to
celebrate him is to think about the value of wisdom and an inquiring
mind like his. If our faith is built on the rock of God's truth, investigat-
ing it further can only strengthen it, as we relish the deep wonders of
God's grace. We should never fear that it will wither under scrutiny:

> ... doubt wisely; in strange way
> To stand inquiring right, is not to stray;
> To sleep, or run wrong, is. On a huge hill,
> Cragged and steep, Truth stands, and he that will
> Reach her, about must and about must go... (From 'Satyre III')

Donne believes in working out his salvation 'with fear and trembling'
(Philippians 2:12), his anxieties spurring him on:

> ... therefore now do;
> Hard deeds, the body's pains; hard knowledge too
> The mind's endeavours reach, and mysteries
> Are like the sun, dazzling, yet plain to all eyes.

His sermons often have this sense of relentless probing in his approach
to God's truth. He vindicates our attempts, however feeble, to study the
Bible as we, too, press on through 'hard knowledge' and 'the mind's
endeavours'. We can follow in his footsteps, and we will find God.

Collect for John Donne

*Almighty God, who enlightened your Church by the teaching of your
servant John Donne, enrich it evermore with your heavenly grace and raise
up other faithful witnesses who, by their lives and teaching, may proclaim
the truth of your salvation.*

RACHEL BOULDING

Draw mine iron heart

I will never forget thy commandments: for with them thou hast quickened me. I am thine, O save me: for I have sought thy commandments. The ungodly laid wait for me to destroy me: but I will consider thy testimonies. I see that all things come to an end: but thy commandment is exceeding broad.

This type of voice from the Psalms has a distinctive tone: personal, honest and often dramatising its own loneliness in an appeal to God. Donne would have prayed some Psalms every day, so it is not surprising that when he cries out to God, his own voice sounds similar. He matches the psalmist's unflinching focus on his predicament and his refusal to mask his anxiety or anger before God. So, here, the psalmist calls on God to save him, citing God's earlier work with him: 'thou hast quickened me ['given me life' in other translations]. I am thine, O save me' (vv. 93–94). Donne echoes this in his Holy Sonnet XIII:

Thou hast made me, and shall Thy work decay?
Repair me now, for now mine end doth haste…

Yet he goes beyond the psalm, beyond its simple pleas for help, vividly portraying both his fears and his utter dependence on God:

Despair behind, and Death before doth cast
Such terror, and my feeble flesh doth waste
By sin in it, which it towards hell doth weigh;
Only Thou art above, and when towards Thee
By Thy leave I can look, I rise again…

Like many of the Psalms that end by expressing their confidence in God, Donne's poem rises to a conclusion that inspires us and points us to the Lord's mercies. Donne manages to be both poignant and stirring ('his art' below refers to the devil's wiles, and 'adamant' is a magnet):

Thy grace may wing me to prevent his art,
And thou like adamant draw mine iron heart.

Reflection

Why do I find it so hard to be honest with God about my fears?

RACHEL BOULDING

The sexual Christian

Ye are the salt of the earth: but if the salt have lost his savour, wherewith shall it be salted? it is thenceforth good for nothing, but to be cast out, and to be trodden under foot of men.

The passages I have quoted so far give a one-sided, even false impression of John Donne. I have referred to his religious works, but he is better known as a love poet, the author of some of the most fiery, passionate—even smutty—lines in English literature. He celebrates sexual expression in the most explicit ways:

Licence my roving hands, and let them go
Before, behind, between, above, below. (Elegy XIX)

Many of these poems are written along established lines at the time (for example, the poem urging a woman to consummate her relationship with the writer was a standard type), but Donne's seem to go beyond exercises in the art of persuasion! So, in these lines from 'The Sun Rising', we have an example of an 'aubade'—a verse about lovers who have to part at dawn. (Shakespeare writes, in *Romeo and Juliet*, 'Night's candles are burnt out, and jocund day / Stands tiptoe on the misty mountain tops.') Donne's version has its own compelling life:

Busy old fool, unruly Sun,
Why dost thou thus,
Through windows, and through curtains, call on us? …
Love, all alike, no season knows, nor clime,
Nor hours, days, months, which are the rags of time…

Donne used all his talents to revel in physicality and later brought the same fervour to his love for God. Just as 'muscular Christians' are often seen as role-models for attracting young people to church, he might just encourage some to realise that faith is not all milk-and-water with the 'pale Galilean'.

Prayer
Father, draw us towards a sense of the fullness of your gifts,
physical and spiritual.

RACHEL BOULDING

Devout fits come and go away

I do not understand my own actions. For I do not do what I want, but I do the very thing I hate. Now if I do what I do not want, I agree that the law is good. But in fact it is no longer I that do it, but sin that dwells within me. For I know that nothing good dwells within me, that is, in my flesh.

One aspect of Donne's sense of wholeness—physical, mental and spiritual—is his refusal to settle for anything less than the truth. He probes his own motivation, exposing the flaws that most of us dare not confront. As we have seen, he is riven by inner conflict. Perhaps he is a more extreme example than most, but we can all relate to this, as we can to this passage from Romans, where Paul dramatises the struggle.

We can all have good intentions, but putting them into practice is so much harder—a situation that Donne encapsulates:

Oh, to vex me, contraries meet in one:
Inconstancy unnaturally hath begot
A constant habit; that when I would not
I change in vows, and in devotion…
So my devout fits come and go away
Like a fantastic ague: save that here
Those are my best days, when I shake with fear. (Holy Sonnet XIX)

The priest and author Mark Oakley describes this opening as the 'one line in Donne's poetry which got me hooked on him for life'. Donne's relentless seeking after the deep resonances of our innermost contradictions, he says, 'has helped me and many others through our ministry by keeping us honest about these things—and more than honest, also unashamed, because such things are more important than being seduced by quick clarity and sound-bite theology… As you read him, you often feel something coming to birth in you.' Thus, Donne can shine light on our most hidden questions and fears.

Prayer

Father, let me rest in your love and rejoice in your care for me, even in the midst of my fears and contradictions.

Rachel Boulding

I neglect God and his Angels

I can will what is right, but I cannot do it. For I do not do the good I want, but the evil I do not want is what I do. Now if I do what I do not want, it is no longer I that do it, but sin that dwells within me. So I find it to be a law that when I want to do what is good, evil lies close at hand.

Another part of the inner conflicts that we noted yesterday, especially in carrying out our good intentions, is the way most of us are so easily distracted at prayer. Whether it is in church or in our quiet times at home, our minds wander. There are some remarkable individuals who do not seem troubled by this, but they are rare.

Donne expresses our frustration in a sermon: 'I call in, and invite God, and his Angels thither, and when they are there, I neglect God and his Angels, for the noise of a fly, for the rattling of a coach, for the whining of a door... A memory of yesterday's pleasures, a fear of tomorrow's dangers, a straw under my knee, noise in mine ear, a light in mine eye, an anything, a nothing, a fancy, a chimera in my brain, troubles me in my prayer. So certainly is there nothing, nothing in spiritual things, perfect in this world.'

He draws a picture of comfort, too, however, assuring us in a later sermon that Jesus will pray with us and in us. It is easy to fall prey to the temptation to give up and leave praying to 'religious professionals'. With perseverance, though, times of prayer really can be the still centre of our lives—no matter how easily distracted we are. If, Donne says, having 'entered into thy prayer, thou have found thyself withdrawn, transported, strayed into some deviations, and by-thoughts; thou must not think all that devotion lost' for God 'will also spread that zeal with which thou enteredest into thy prayer, over thy whole prayer, and where that (thine own zeal) is too short, Christ Jesus himself will spread his prayer over thine, and say, "Give him, O Father, that which he hath asked faithfully in my name, and, where he hath fallen into any deviations or negligences, Father forgive him."'

Prayer
Father, take my distractions and draw the whole of me towards you.

RACHEL BOULDING

Constant and cheerful resolution

I have yet many things to say unto you, but ye cannot bear them now. Howbeit when he, the Spirit of truth, is come, he will guide you into all truth: for he shall not speak of himself; but whatsoever he shall hear, that shall he speak: and he will shew you things to come. He shall glorify me: for he shall receive of mine, and shall shew it unto you.

During this past couple of weeks, we have glanced at Donne's relentless probing and passionate approach to life, love and God. Unlike so many of us, he manages to look death in the face and, while still feeling his fears, assert that its sting has indeed been overcome.

When he knew he was dying, Donne made his will (on St Lucy's Day, 13 December 1630—perhaps relishing the date, as he had marked it in one of his greatest poems, 'A Nocturnal upon S. Lucy's Day'). With his usual sense of bringing together his whole self as an offering to God, he wrote: 'I give my good and gracious God an entire Sacrifice of Body and Soul with my most humble thanks for that assurance which his blessed Spirit imprints in me now of the Salvation of the one and the Resurrection of the other.' A few weeks later, Donne preached his final sermon (now known as 'Death's Duel'), in which he was his unflinching self about what awaited him: 'truly a death and truly a resurrection… this death of corruption and putrefaction, of vermiculation and incineration'.

He ended the sermon with a characteristic marriage of physicality and faithful conviction: 'There we leave you in that blessed dependency, to hang upon him that hangs upon the cross, there bathe in his tears, there suck at his wounds, and lie down in peace in his grave, till he vouchsafe you a resurrection, and an ascension into that kingdom which He hath prepared for you with the inestimable price of his incorruptible blood. Amen.'

Prayer

God of truth… help us to lay aside all foolishness and to live and walk in the way of insight, that we may come with John Donne to the eternal feast of heaven. Amen

From the post-Communion prayer for the commemoration of John Donne,
Common Worship
RACHEL BOULDING

Jesus the Messiah

As we approach Holy Week and prepare to celebrate Easter itself, our readings are taken from Matthew's Gospel, following the journey of Jesus towards Calvary. We begin at Caesarea Philippi (16:13), with the great revelation that Jesus is the Messiah, the Christ of whom the prophets spoke, the one long awaited in Israel.

We will follow the journey closely as Jesus and his followers return to Galilee (17:22), then move south to the part of Judea across the Jordan (19:1), before heading for the last time to Jerusalem (20:17). There we see him entering the temple area daily from his base in Bethany (21:12, 17), before his arrest in Gethsemane and subsequent trial in the city. Then we watch as he stumbles towards Golgotha and crucifixion, before we share the joy of Mary and others in the garden as the realisation dawns that he is alive again.

This will not only be a geographical journey but also a spiritual one as we ponder anew what it meant that he was to be a suffering Messiah. We will see the bewilderment of his friends as he repeatedly explains what is to happen to him in Jerusalem. We will feel the growing hostility of his enemies as their determination to get rid of him intensifies. We will marvel at the strength of his calling to do the Father's will regardless of the suffering involved. We will find ourselves rejoicing at the triumph of his resurrection.

Some readers will have walked the road to Calvary like this many times before and be aware how familiarity with the story can rob it of its power. Others may be coming to it with fresh eyes, struggling to make sense of it all and keep track of the details. Either way, pray that God will make the story live to you, for here are sacred truths deep at the heart of our faith.

I have selected only certain passages from Matthew 16—28, which I hope convey the sense of movement and unfolding drama as the story is told. You may want to read more widely around the passages for the complete story.

Tony Horsfall

Who do you say I am?

When Jesus came to the region of Caesarea Philippi, he asked his disciples, 'Who do people say the Son of Man is?' They replied, 'Some say John the Baptist; others say Elijah; and still others, Jeremiah or one of the prophets.' 'But what about you?' he asked. 'Who do you say I am?' Simon Peter answered, 'You are the Messiah, the Son of the living God.' Jesus replied, 'Blessed are you, Simon son of Jonah, for this was not revealed to you by flesh and blood, but by my Father in heaven.'

This is a watershed moment in the Gospel accounts of the life of Jesus. The first half of the story has introduced us to this remarkable person who teaches with authority, heals the sick, performs amazing miracles and lives a holy life, but who is he?

We see the disciples volunteer several popular answers to this question, but none of them is correct. The disciples have been with him for many months now and have had the privilege of watching him closely and asking him their own questions. Not surprisingly, Jesus now asks them a pointed question regarding his identity. It is Peter who responds, perhaps because he is the most outspoken or the others are less confident. 'You are the Messiah, the Son of the living God' (v. 16), he asserts with conviction. It is an amazing declaration, a recognition reflecting profound spiritual insight that is not the product of his own intelligence but has been given him by God. What others, more educated and more religiously schooled, could not see, Peter was enabled to grasp with clarity: Jesus is the long-awaited Messiah, the One of whom the Old Testament prophets had spoken and for whom all Israel was waiting.

This declaration of the true identity of Jesus leads us into the second half of the story, where the focus shifts towards Calvary and his impending death. Jesus' response remains, however, and his question is a very personal one: 'But what about you? … Who do you say I am?' (v. 15). The answer will come not from intellectual analysis alone but also from spiritual revelation.

Prayer

Lord, open my eyes so I can grasp the true identity of Jesus.

TONY HORSFALL

A suffering Messiah

From that time on Jesus began to explain to his disciples that he must go to Jerusalem and suffer many things at the hands of the elders, the chief priests and the teachers of the law, and that he must be killed and on the third day be raised to life. Peter took him aside and began to rebuke him. 'Never, Lord!' he said. 'This shall never happen to you!' Jesus turned and said to Peter, 'Get behind me, Satan!'

'From that time on' (v. 21) indicates that Peter's recognition of the Messiahship of Jesus was a turning point as far as Jesus was concerned. Now he will begin to prepare himself and his disciples for what lies ahead and face the future with courage and determination.

It would have been easy for Jesus to allow his followers to incorporate popular notions of a political Messiah into their understanding of who he was and what he had come to do, but his mission was not to liberate them from their Roman masters or any other oppressive power; his calling was to bring about a spiritual liberation and for that he needed to become a suffering Messiah.

We can see already how clearly Jesus perceives his future and his destiny. There is inevitability about what will happen, a divine necessity that is at work ('must go... must be killed', v. 21). The climax will take place in Jerusalem and the human source of his suffering will come from the religious leaders who have opposed him from the beginning. Tragedy will turn to triumph, however, because, although he will be put to death, on the third day he will be raised to life. Peter's moment of sublime insight now turns to the darkest misunderstanding that threatens to deflect his Master from his heavenly calling. Perhaps it is the emotion of protective love that clouds his judgment, even as later it will move him to take up a sword in defence of his friend (John 18:10).

Reflection

It is never easy to accept the path of suffering as one chosen for us by God. Everything within us wants to avoid it, for ourselves and others. Sometimes, though, it is the only way.

TONY HORSFALL

The transfiguration

After six days Jesus took with him Peter, James and John the brother of James, and led them up a high mountain by themselves. There he was transfigured before them. His face shone like the sun, and his clothes became as white as the light. Just then there appeared before them Moses and Elijah, talking with Jesus… While [Peter] was still speaking, a bright cloud covered them, and a voice from the cloud said, 'This is my Son, whom I love; with him I am well pleased. Listen to him!'

Shortly after the momentous declaration at Caesarea Philippi comes an event of equally great significance. Jesus takes with him the inner group of Peter, James and John and is transfigured before them.

For most of his time on earth Jesus' heavenly glory was veiled and the true splendour of his being hidden from view. He appeared like every other man, without distinguishing marks to betray his divine origin. Now, however, for a brief moment, the curtain is pulled back and the full reality of who he is allowed to shine forth.

Presumably this takes place for the benefit of the disciples and to strengthen their faith in him as the Messiah and the Son of God. It certainly has a deep impact on them as, awestruck, they fall to the ground. Jesus comes to them tenderly and touches them (v. 7), telling them not to be afraid. Peter, for his part, never forgot this sacred moment when he was eye-witness to the glory of Jesus (2 Peter 1:16–18).

The voice from heaven is also for the disciples' benefit as it calls them to listen to Jesus, but, I would suggest, it is equally beneficial for Jesus. This heavenly affirmation, in line with that given at his baptism (Matthew 3:17), again underlines his identity as the Son and reminds him of the Father's love and approval. I believe that Jesus needed to hear such words as he prepared for what lay ahead of him in Jerusalem and would have received tremendous strength and encouragement from hearing the Father's voice at such a crucial moment.

Prayer
Father, may I listen to your Son and see his glory.

TONY HORSFALL

The lost sheep

[Jesus said] 'What do you think? If a man owns a hundred sheep, and one of them wanders away, will he not leave the ninety-nine on the hills and go to look for the one that wandered off? And if he finds it, truly I tell you, he is happier about that one sheep than about the ninety-nine that did not wander off. In the same way your Father in heaven is not willing that any of these little ones should perish.'

The Gospel accounts do not tell us much about why Jesus died. They are content to record the events and describe what happened. The theological explanation of his death is largely left to the epistles and to Paul in particular. In this little parable, however, we begin to learn something about how Jesus understood his mission and the reason for his death that later writers built on.

Matthew places the parable in the context of the love of Jesus for the little children (v. 10), whereas Luke puts his fuller version in the setting of the accusation that Jesus welcomes sinners (Luke 15:1–7). Obviously he could have told the parable more than once and adapted it according to the audience. The essence remains the same: Jesus is the Shepherd who has come, at the Father's behest, to find the one sheep that has gone missing (young or old) and does so at personal cost.

Peter is one of the writers who builds on this idea. 'For you were like sheep going astray,' he writes, 'but now you have returned to the Shepherd and Overseer of your souls' (1 Peter 2:25). This wandering or going astray is equated with our sinfulness, our turning aside to go our own selfish way (Isaiah 53:6).

The coming back to the fold is made possible only because the penalty of sin is dealt with by the Shepherd laying down his life for the sheep. As Peter says, 'He himself bore our sins in his body on the tree' (1 Peter 2:24). Once again there is a challenge to assess our personal situation: 'What do you think?'

Prayer

*Lord, thank you that you search for us, even when we have
wilfully gone astray.*

TONY HORSFALL

Let the children come

> Then people brought little children to Jesus for him to place his
> hands on them and pray for them. But the disciples rebuked
> them. Jesus said, 'Let the little children come to me, and do not
> hinder them, for the kingdom of heaven belongs to such as these.'
> When he had placed his hands on them, he went on from there.

Children continue to figure prominently in Matthew's writing at this
point in his Gospel and for two reasons. First, Jesus loves the little
children and has time for them. When other grown-ups find them an
inconvenience and distraction, he chooses to bless them and pray for
them. Surely this underlines for us the importance of ministry towards
children and young people. At a time when young people are leaving
our churches in droves, here is a reminder that we cannot sit back and
do nothing. Initiatives like Messy Church have transformed the ability
of smaller congregations to reach not just children but also whole families. My own church fellowship, despite the advancing years of some,
has been revitalised by putting an emphasis on this form of outreach.
The work of Barnabas in Schools and other similar organisations is,
likewise, worthy of our prayer and practical support.

Second, Jesus says that if we are to feel at home in his kingdom we
must become like little children. He does not mean, of course, that we
are to be childish, but we should be childlike in our approach to spiritual things—trusting, responsive, simple and uncomplicated, sponta-
neous and unselfconscious. It is sad how complicated we can become
as we grow as Christians and find ourselves involved in the issues of
church life. Somewhere along the way, we lose our spiritual innocence
and become guarded and defensive rather than open and vulnerable.

Perhaps further growth in our spiritual life might require a rediscov-
ery of the freedom and receptivity that we once knew, a return to that
'first naiveté' of simple, childlike faith. Maybe it could start today if you
imagine yourself coming to Jesus like a child and asking him to place
his hands of blessing on you.

Reflection

'When he had placed his hands on them, he went on from there' (v. 15).

TONY HORSFALL

Jesus predicts his death

Now Jesus was going up to Jerusalem. On the way, he took the Twelve aside and said to them, 'We are going up to Jerusalem, and the Son of Man will be delivered over to the chief priests and the teachers of the law. They will condemn him to death and will hand him over to the Gentiles to be mocked and flogged and crucified. On the third day he will be raised to life!'

For a second time Jesus speaks openly about his death. On this occasion, he takes the disciples aside privately and instructs them about what will happen. They are now heading for Jerusalem and the journey to Calvary has begun in earnest.

What he tells them first is that he will be 'delivered over' to the religious authorities. Here is the first indication that it will be through betrayal that his fate will be sealed. This becomes clearer as time goes on and the role of Judas becomes plain for all to see (26:14–16, 23–24, 47–50; 27:3–5). It is not something that takes Jesus by surprise, although it does disappoint him deeply. He still washes the betrayer's feet and still shares the bread and wine with him—such is the Saviour's love for his own. Jesus also spells out the nature of the suffering to come. He will be mocked, flogged and crucified, the shameful execution of a common criminal that brings with it the condemnation of God— 'anyone who is hung on a tree is under God's curse' (Deuteronomy 21:23; Galatians 3:13, NRSV).

There is still a joyful note of resurrection here, but we can only imagine the confusion there must have been in the minds of the disciples as they tried to fathom what their Master was saying. This time there is no outburst in protest from Peter, but inwardly they must have wondered, 'How can this be?' and 'Why would such a thing happen?'

We stand on this side of Calvary and we know in part the answers to both questions, but still the mystery of it and the injustice behind it confounds us.

Reflection

Amazing love! How can it be that thou, my God, shouldst die for me?

Charles Wesley, 1739

TONY HORSFALL

A ransom for many

Jesus called [the disciples] together and said, 'You know that the rulers of the Gentiles lord it over them, and their high officials exercise authority over them. Not so with you. Instead, whoever wants to become great among you must be your servant, and whoever wants to be first must be your slave—just as the Son of Man did not come to be served, but to serve, and to give his life as a ransom for many.'

The outline of forthcoming events that we looked at yesterday is followed immediately by a rather insensitive and selfish request from the mother of James and John that her sons should have the seats of honour in the coming kingdom (v. 21). She has neither understood the nature of the kingdom nor the way in which it will come into being. The indignant response of the other disciples prompts Jesus to explain further the radical nature of discipleship.

The pattern for life in the kingdom is the life of Jesus himself and he did not come looking for prominence and power (to be served) but, rather, to give his life on behalf of others (to serve). The word used to describe his death—a 'ransom'—suggests the freeing of a slave by making a payment. This is the spiritual liberation that a suffering Messiah will accomplish by his death—freedom from the penalty and power of sin.

With this as the foundation stone, life in the kingdom will be characterised by servanthood. It will be in complete contrast to the power structures of worldly kingdoms. In Christ's kingdom, greatness is measured by the willingness to serve others. The motivation is love and the chief characteristic is humility.

This is why Christian leadership is often described as servant leadership as it is not about position and power but helping and enabling others. The more we understand the cross, the more we will be liberated from the self-centredness that is ambitious for position and grasping power. The greater our understanding of what he has done for us, the greater will be our willingness to serve, sacrificially.

Prayer

Lord, grant me grace today to serve gladly and with humility.

TONY HORSFALL

The triumphal entry

Jesus sent two disciples, saying to them, 'Go to the village ahead of you, and at once you will find a donkey tied there, with her colt by her. Untie them and bring them to me...' This took place to fulfil what was spoken through the prophet: 'Say to Daughter Zion, "See, your king comes to you, gentle and riding on a donkey, and on a colt, the foal of a donkey."'

Matthew is writing for a mainly Jewish audience and his aim is to demonstrate that Jesus is the Messiah, although not the political Messiah that many expected. His chief way of convincing his readers of the true identity of Jesus is by constantly showing how the events in his life fulfilled Old Testament scriptures. The way he chose to enter the city of Jerusalem is a case in point.

Whereas most political leaders (Roman generals, for example) would display their power by making a grand entrance on a white stallion, Jesus chose a more humble mount—he came riding a donkey. The symbolism was not lost on Matthew, even if others did not fully realise what was happening. For Matthew, this was a clear and literal fulfilment of the prophecy of Zechariah (9:9), further proof that Jesus was indeed the Messiah, the true 'king' of Israel.

Such a low-key entrance is in keeping with the character of the Messiah (lowly and gentle) and the nature of his kingdom (unpretentious and without ostentation). This suffering Messiah will not triumph either by the force of his personality or the strength of his army, but through humility and love and the laying down of his life.

Palm Sunday is thus a reminder to us of another of Zechariah's insights into the coming of the kingdom: '"Not by might nor by power, but by my Spirit," says the Lord' (4:6). It has always been a temptation for the church to seek to triumph by adopting secular methods and political strategies and to value status, power and wealth above spiritual anointing. If today teaches us anything, it is that Jesus walked a different path and invites us to do the same.

Meditation

'"Who is this?"... "This is Jesus"' (Matthew 21:10–11).

TONY HORSFALL

Anointed for burial

Jesus said to [the disciples], 'Why are you bothering this woman? She has done a beautiful thing to me. The poor you will always have with you, but you will not always have me. When she poured this perfume on my body, she did it to prepare me for burial. Truly I tell you, wherever this gospel is preached throughout the world, what she has done will also be told, in memory of her.'

Some years ago, Malcolm Muggeridge wrote a book about Mother Teresa's life and work in Calcutta, called *Something Beautiful for God*. He was deeply affected by the demonstration of Christlike love that he encountered in her work among the poor. Perhaps he took the title from this Bible passage, which describes a loving act of great devotion to Jesus.

Although Matthew does not name the woman who anoints Jesus, it is generally assumed to have been Mary Magdalene, the one from whom Jesus had cast out many demons (Luke 8:2). Whoever she was, she was not afraid to express publicly and extravagantly her love for the Master. According to Mark, this perfume was not only rare but also expensive, worth more than a year's wages (Mark 14:5). Such extravagance provoked indignation from those present, including the disciples. In hard economic terms, it was a waste; even in ministry terms the money could have been used for the poor. Yet, Jesus commends her actions, does not rebuke her and assures her of a place in gospel history.

This act of unrestrained love and expression of devotion ministered to him deeply at a moment when he needed to receive encouragement from others. Perhaps even the simple gift of touch communicated strength to him at a time when he was soon to experience the sting of a friend's betrayal and the fierce hostility of his enemies. In some significant way, her action prepared him for what was to come.

Cold logic will never understand loving devotion, but, as Jesus said elsewhere, those who have been forgiven much will love much (Luke 7:47). We should never be afraid of being extravagant in our love for him.

Prayer
Lord, may I also do something beautiful for you.

TONY HORSFALL

119

The Last Supper

While they were eating, Jesus took bread, and when he had given thanks, he broke it and gave it to his disciples, saying, 'Take and eat; this is my body.' Then he took a cup, and when he had given thanks, he gave it to them, saying, 'Drink from it, all of you. This is my blood of the covenant, which is poured out for many for the forgiveness of sins.'

At the start of the Jewish Passover, we reflect on the Passover meal that Jesus shared with his disciples and which now forms the basis for us of Holy Communion.

In Jewish culture, a meal is more than simply an opportunity to consume food. It is an occasion for friendship and conversation, a sharing of life together. As such, for Jesus, too, this time with his closest friends must have been very special. As the shadow of the cross falls darkly over him, I feel sure he simply enjoyed their companionship and the fun and laughter of kindred spirits.

The setting also provides a visual aid for Jesus to instruct them even further in the meaning of his approaching death. The bread speaks of his body that will be broken and the cup of wine of his blood that will be shed. Together, they disclose something of the mystery of what his death will achieve.

It will establish a new covenant. Through his death on the cross he will bring into effect an entirely new way of relating to God, not based on human achievement in keeping the law but on the outcome of his death. What is that? The forgiveness of sins. In a way that will be later explained more fully by Paul and others, the death of Jesus will deal with the problem of human alienation from God because of sin. To use a theological term, it will provide atonement, make it possible for sin to be forgiven.

Forgiveness is something that we all need as we have all sinned. We do not need to struggle with shame and guilt for what we have done as we can be forgiven, completely and forever, because of his death.

Reflection
His death brings forgiveness, full and free.

TONY HORSFALL

Gethsemane

Going a little farther, [Jesus] fell with his face to the ground and prayed, 'My Father, if it is possible, may this cup be taken from me. Yet not as I will, but as you will.' Then he returned to his disciples and found them sleeping. 'Couldn't you men keep watch with me for one hour?' he asked Peter. 'Watch and pray so that you will not fall into temptation. The spirit is willing, but the flesh is weak.'

Never think that Jesus found it easy to go to the cross. Yes, he was determined and displayed a steadfast intensity that frightened the disciples as they set off towards Jerusalem for the final time (Mark 9:32). Yet, as we have seen, he needed the affirmation of his heavenly Father (Matthew 17:5), appreciated the loving gesture of the anointing at Bethany (26:12) and took comfort from the companionship of his friends as the time drew near (v. 18). Here we see just how agonising his final step was.

Jesus says that his soul is 'overwhelmed with sorrow to the point of death' (v. 38) and he cannot have been exaggerating the inner anguish he must have felt as he contemplated the horrors of the cross. As a man, he must have shrunk from the physical pain involved in crucifixion and from the abuse and scorn that would be heaped on him; as the pure Son of God he must have recoiled at the thought of bearing the sin of the world and being separated from his heavenly Father.

When he most needs support from his closest friends, he is let down. Presently he will be betrayed with a kiss. This is a lonely, heartbreaking moment when, briefly, he wonders if there is another way… but it is only briefly. Almost as soon as the thought surfaces, his inner resolve to do the Father's will takes over and he offers himself again: 'Yet not as I will, but as you will' (v. 39).

We cannot but admire him for his courage and love him for his sacrifice and pray that when we face our own Gethsemane, we may have the grace to make his prayer our own.

Reflection
Not my will, but yours.

Tony Horsfall

Barabbas

Now it was the governor's custom at the festival to release a prisoner chosen by the crowd. At that time they had a well-known prisoner whose name was Jesus Barabbas. So when the crowd had gathered, Pilate asked them, 'Which one do you want me to release to you: Jesus Barabbas, or Jesus who is called the Messiah?'... 'Barabbas,' they answered. 'What shall I do, then, with Jesus who is called the Messiah?' Pilate asked. They all answered, 'Crucify him!'... Then he released Barabbas to them. But he had Jesus flogged, and handed him over to be crucified.

The betrayal of Judas is followed by the denial of Peter, the arrest and interrogation at the house of Caiaphas (the high priest), and an appearance before Pilate (the Roman Governor). Legal irregularities abound and injustice is taking place, yet Jesus remains calm and at peace.

Pilate is no fool and knows the charges against Jesus are false, motivated by envy (v. 18). Furthermore, his wife has an intuitive sense that Jesus is innocent and warns her husband accordingly (v. 19). Mindful of the delicate political balance over which he presides, Pilate seeks a way of compromise that will relieve him of making a decision. It was his custom at Passover to release a prisoner to pacify the Jewish people, so he offers them a choice: should he release Barabbas or Jesus?

We made reference earlier to the excitable nature of the crowd and now, incited by their religious leaders and motivated by religious fervour and group mentality, they turn against Jesus, asking for Barabbas to be set free. So it is that a guilty criminal is released and the innocent Son of God is taken to be crucified.

This story seems to illustrate perfectly a central aspect of the cross— that of substitution. Not only did Jesus take the place of Barabbas but he also took the place of each one of us, for he died instead of us. Because he took our place, we have been set free.

Reflection

Bearing shame and scoffing rude, In my place condemned he stood;
Sealed my pardon with his blood: Hallelujah! What a Saviour!

Philip Bliss, 1875

TONY HORSFALL

The crucifixion

Two rebels were crucified with him, one on his right and one on his left. Those who passed by hurled insults at him, shaking their heads and saying, 'You who are going to destroy the temple and build it in three days, save yourself! Come down from the cross, if you are the Son of God!' In the same way the chief priests, the teachers of the law and the elders mocked him. 'He saved others,' they said, 'but he can't save himself!'

On this most holy of days, we pause to read Matthew's account of the crucifixion and stand again beneath the cross of Jesus.

We stand here in worship, for what can stir the heart of a believer more than to see the innocent Saviour dying such a cruel and ignominious death? Here he is, counted among the guilty and condemned, the criminal and the rebel, the worst of all offenders. Here he dies, not for his own sin, but for yours and mine, that we might be brought back to God. As we watch, love rises in our hearts and grateful worship forms on our lips.

We stand here in wonder, for who can fully understand the mystery of what is taking place? Human words and explanations will never adequately convey exactly how it is that this cruel death can be the means of salvation for fallen humankind. Sometimes, though, we need no words, faith being content to trust, to believe, to accept that which God says is happening. Hushed silence is the best response.

Save himself? Of course he cannot save himself! He dies to save the world. We stand here in witness to that, aligning ourselves with him and bearing testimony to what he has done in our lives. Others may scoff and ridicule and pour scorn on him, but we identify with him. In a post-Christian world, Jesus and those who follow him are increasingly marginalised and likely to be objects of disdain. Sometimes even the symbol of the cross itself appears to give offence. It requires courage these days to stand with Jesus and follow in his steps.

Prayer

Thank you, Jesus! Your death has brought us life.

TONY HORSFALL

The burial

As evening approached, there came a rich man from Arimathea, named Joseph, who had himself become a disciple of Jesus. Going to Pilate, he asked for Jesus' body, and Pilate ordered that it be given to him. Joseph took the body, wrapped it in a clean linen cloth, and placed it in his own new tomb that he had cut out of the rock. He rolled a big stone in front of the entrance to the tomb and went away.

Joseph displays immense courage, identifying himself so clearly as being with Jesus—remember that the disciples had all deserted and fled (26:56) and even the women are watching from a safe distance (27:55). Strong feelings have been released and there is danger in the air. In this climate, it is a bold move to approach Pilate and ask for Jesus' body.

We are told that Joseph, as well as being a wealthy man, was already a follower of Jesus. Mark notes that he is a highly respected member of the Sanhedrin (15:43), but, according to Luke, not consenting to their decisions about Jesus (Luke 23:51). John adds that he had been a secret follower until this point because he feared the Jewish leaders, and did not go alone but with his friend Nicodemus (John 19:38–39). Clearly the cross brought him to a crossroads and he chose to go forward boldly in discipleship rather than backwards in cowardice.

Joseph's generosity is demonstrated in bringing the body of Jesus for burial to his own unused tomb, thereby including Jesus within his family. His love for the Master is shown in his purchase of linen cloth with which to wrap the body and anointing it with expensive spices, then following carefully the Jewish burial customs (John 19:39–40). Such a tender display of affection reminds us of the anointing at Bethany and illustrates the depth of devotion that Jesus inspired in his followers.

There is one final, thoughtful act. Joseph ensures that the tomb is safe by rolling a large stone across the entrance to keep out wild animals and graverobbers. Courage, generosity, tenderness and care are the marks of Joseph's discipleship—qualities worthy of emulation today.

Prayer
Lord, I, too, would follow bravely.

TONY HORSFALL

The resurrection

After the Sabbath, at dawn on the first day of the week, Mary Magdalene and the other Mary went to look at the tomb... The angel said to the women, 'Do not be afraid, for I know that you are looking for Jesus, who was crucified. He is not here; he has risen, just as he said. Come and see the place where he lay. Then go quickly and tell his disciples: "He has risen from the dead and is going ahead of you into Galilee. There you will see him." Now I have told you.'

If Good Friday is the most holy of days, Easter Day is surely the most joyful. Throughout the world today, as the sun rises over our planet, believers of all nationalities and backgrounds will rise early and excitedly to declare together, 'Christ is risen! He is risen indeed!'

The resurrection stands at the heart of our faith and is the reason for our confidence. If Christ had died and remained dead, we would have no assurance that his death had accomplished anything. The fact that he came back to life and appeared to his followers is the guarantee that his work had been effective: sin has been dealt with, Satan has been defeated and death has been conquered.

At its heart, Christianity is simple. The things of crucial importance are these: 'that Christ died for our sins according to the scriptures, that he was buried, that he was raised on the third day according to the scriptures' (1 Corinthians 15:3–4). This is what we are to believe and what we are to proclaim.

So, today, allow that sense of joy and victory to permeate your thoughts and feelings, lift your spirits and inspire you to worship jubilantly. Live with a sense that the risen Christ is with you, has overcome the world and so can you. He said he would rise again and he did. Let this glad assurance strengthen your faith and give confidence to your witness. Remember this: the same Spirit that raised Christ Jesus from the dead now lives in you (Romans 8:11).

Prayer

Christ, the Lord, is risen today, Alleluia!

Charles Wesley, 1739

TONY HORSFALL

After Pentecost: Acts 25—26

We have reached the penultimate chapters of the book of Acts in the series, 'After Pentecost'. God's Holy Spirit has been poured out on all Christian believers. Churches have been established and persecution has been rife. Paul has been in prison for two years and now has occasion to tell his story to Festus, the new Roman governor. Festus is unfamiliar with the religion and culture of Judea and wants to curry favour with the religious leaders. He does not realise, however, that these people want to assassinate Paul and offers Paul an opportunity to go to Jerusalem. Paul declines and, instead, opts to 'appeal to Caesar' (Acts 25:11), as he is a Roman citizen. In desperation Festus invites King Agrippa, a political leader of the Jewish faith, to offer advice. Paul, in chains, makes his longest recorded speech before Festus and Agrippa. They find no basis for any charges against him, but because Paul has appealed to the emperor, he is sent to Rome.

As we look at the passages in more detail we shall see fascinating contrasts between the personal ambition of political and religious leaders and Paul's commitment to the gospel. An assassination plot is thwarted while an otherwise largely honest man lacks the courage to offer justice and chooses instead to avoid conflict and blame others. A religious leader narrowly avoids conversion to Christ after Paul once again shares the story of his encounter with Jesus on the Damascus road.

We shall see people both intrigued by and terrified of the person of Jesus and Christian faith. We shall encounter those who act in God's name but contrary to God's purposes. We shall come across persecution of the Church and individuals and the effects of becoming a Christian. Above all, we are confronted by Paul's driving passion that every person he meets should become a Christian. Reading Ben Witherington III's commentary on Acts (*The Acts of the Apostles*, Eerdmans, 2001), I have been amazed by the parallels between the individuals in the two chapters we shall study and people today, including ourselves. As you engage with these studies, too, perhaps you will join me in praying that God will continue to forgive, challenge and encourage us as we live in the power of the Holy Spirit.

Lakshmi Jeffries

Who is in charge?

Three days after arriving in the province, Festus went up from Caesarea to Jerusalem, where the chief priests and the Jewish leaders appeared before him and presented the charges against Paul. They requested Festus, as a favour to them, to have Paul transferred to Jerusalem, for they were preparing an ambush to kill him along the way. Festus answered, 'Paul is being held at Caesarea, and I myself am going there soon. Let some of your leaders come with me, and if the man has done anything wrong, they can press charges against him there.'

Porcius Festus was not like his predecessor Felix: he was largely honest and wanted to sort out the anarchic mess he found in Judea as quickly as possible. In fact, only three days after arriving in the province, he had arranged a meeting with the Jewish authorities. He realised that in order to govern effectively he would need the support of the resident communities. He did not understand their religious customs and laws but needed to do so in order to accommodate their traditions within strict Roman law. What better way to curry favour than to help the local leaders resolve a problem with a 'troublemaker' who happened to be a Roman citizen?

Festus, however, was not going to allow anyone to dictate to him. Paul was being held in Caesarea and, as Festus was planning to go there soon, anyone with relevant authority could accompany him to settle the matter. He clearly had no idea that those who came to him hoped to assassinate Paul en route.

Then, as now, our lives are significantly affected by the actions of others, especially those with some form of authority over us. Here, Paul's fate was in the hands of Festus, the new governor. Yet, although not directly mentioned, God was looking after Paul. Festus was not pushed around by anyone and, as a result, the Jewish authorities had to change their immediate plans. Others might have power and influence over us, but, ultimately, our lives are in God's care.

Prayer
Pray for those in positions of government and authority.

LAKSHMI JEFFRIES

Courage of convictions

After spending eight or ten days with them, Festus went down to Caesarea. The next day he convened the court and ordered that Paul be brought before him. When Paul came in, the Jews who had come down from Jerusalem stood round him. They brought many serious charges against him, but they could not prove them. Then Paul made his defence: 'I have done nothing wrong against the Jewish law or against the temple or against Caesar.'

Paul was not in an easy situation. He was surrounded by his enemies who were making lots of serious charges against him, although none of them could be proved. Festus knew nothing about Jewish Law, but recognised that this was not simply a religious problem. Paul was a Roman citizen and this gave the matter a political dimension. Festus had to decide if there was a case to answer and, if so, where, how and by whom. Meanwhile, Paul was adamant that he had done nothing wrong in either religious or political terms (in relation to Jewish law, temple or Caesar).

While it is unwise to make rigid distinctions between 'the world' and God's kingdom, Christians remain 'strangers in the world' (1 Peter 1:1): our true home is with Jesus in the kingdom of God. Paul had no obvious place of belonging. As Festus acknowledged, Paul was a Roman citizen, but he saw him primarily as someone who had upset the religious leaders. Equally, the Jewish authorities viewed Paul as a dangerous maverick to be put to death before he destroyed all they stood for.

There will be times when our faith in Jesus brings us into opposition with those around us and we will wonder where we belong. Some will misunderstand who we are. Others might recognise exactly who we stand for and, for that reason, will want to destroy us, if not physically, then financially or in terms of our reputation. Establishing the kingdom of God cost Jesus his life and might cost Paul his, but each was willing to pay the price because they knew the love of the God to whom they truly belonged.

Prayer

Pray for the Holy Spirit to fill Christians around the world who risk their lives because of faith in Jesus.

LAKSHMI JEFFRIES

Whom do you please?

Festus, wishing to do the Jews a favour, said to Paul, 'Are you willing to go up to Jerusalem and stand trial before me there on these charges?' Paul answered: 'I am now standing before Caesar's court, where I ought to be tried. I have not done any wrong to the Jews, as you yourself know very well. If, however, I am guilty of doing anything deserving death, I do not refuse to die. But if the charges brought against me by these Jews are not true, no one has the right to hand me over to them. I appeal to Caesar!'

Festus might not have been as corrupt as his predecessor, Felix, but he was new in office and wanted to ingratiate himself with the local religious leaders. This was clearly a concern of Jewish rather than Roman law. By sending Paul to Jerusalem, Festus would rid himself of the problem, win the favour of the local Jewish leaders and generally be well thought of in the province and beyond. The one obstacle Festus faced was that, although there were relatively few Jewish people who were also Roman citizens, Paul's citizenship meant that Festus could not compel him to go to Jerusalem.

Wisely, Paul did not trust Festus: he knew that he would not receive justice in Jerusalem, assuming he ever even reached the city. In addition, he knew that not only had he done nothing wrong but also Festus was aware of Paul's innocence. Paul therefore appealed to the emperor, the highest Roman authority.

Festus lacked the courage to act justly—that is, release Paul and risk the wrath of the religious leaders. It is often tempting to try to appease those who shout loudest or appear most powerful. Paul wrote: 'Am I now seeking human approval, or God's approval? Or am I trying to please people? If I were still pleasing people, I would not be a servant of Christ' (Galatians 1:10, NRSV). Others are always affected by our actions, so how shall we choose?

Reflection

What does the Lord require of you but to act justly, love mercy and walk humbly with your God? (Micah 6:8)

LAKSHMI JEFFRIES

The beauty of spin

A few days later King Agrippa and Bernice arrived at Caesarea to pay their respects to Festus... Festus discussed Paul's case with the king. He said: 'There is a man here whom Felix left as a prisoner. When I went to Jerusalem, the chief priests and the elders of the Jews brought charges against him and asked that he be condemned... They had some points of dispute with him about their own religion and about a dead man named Jesus whom Paul claimed was alive... I asked if he would be willing to go to Jerusalem and stand trial there on these charges... Paul made his appeal to be held over for the Emperor's decision.'

Things had not been going as well as Festus might have hoped up until these important visitors arrived. King Agrippa was the son of Herod, who killed John the Baptist (Matthew 14:1–10). Bernice was his sister and consort and there were rumours of an incestuous relationship. They were prominent Jewish people, and favourites of the Roman authorities.

Festus is keen to impress them so presents his dilemma from his own viewpoint, systematically blaming others for the problem: Felix had not dealt with the matter; Paul's accusers were incompetent; Paul did not want to go to Jerusalem. Festus also puts a positive spin on his own actions, giving the impression that he has acted swiftly to resolve the problem and is a humble man who knows his limitations. Nothing he says is strictly untrue, but his account is, at the least, biased, showing that he is concerned only for his reputation, irrespective of justice for Paul.

How easy it is to present ourselves in the best possible light and, in the process, diminish others! Sin can be defined as putting ourselves first, failing to give that place to God. The more we trust God's love for us, especially when life is complicated, the more we are able to put God and others' needs before our personal standing. Our model is Jesus, who 'did not come to be served, but to serve, and to give his life as a ransom for many' (Matthew 20:28).

Prayer
Forgive me, Lord, when I present my version of events and forget that Jesus is the truth.

LAKSHMI JEFFRIES

In the face of injustice

Then Agrippa said to Festus, 'I would like to hear this man myself.'... The next day Agrippa and Bernice came... with the high-ranking military officers and the prominent men of the city. At the command of Festus, Paul was brought in. Festus said: 'King Agrippa... you see this man! The whole Jewish community has petitioned me about him in Jerusalem and here in Caesarea, shouting that he ought not to live any longer. I found he had done nothing deserving of death, but because he made his appeal to the Emperor I decided to send him to Rome... I have brought him before all of you... so that as a result of this investigation I may have something to write. For I think it is unreasonable to send a prisoner on to Rome without specifying the charges against him.'

This is a grand occasion: all the important people are in their finery. Festus is at the centre, claiming that the whole Jewish community in Jerusalem and Caesarea has petitioned him about Paul, hence the need for Agrippa. As Paul has not done anything against Roman law, however, Festus has nothing to write to the emperor about Paul. It would be fatal to Festus' career for him to appear to be wasting the emperor's time, so Festus asks for Agrippa's help in composing a relevant document.

In fact, Festus would not have had this problem if he had been courageous enough simply to dismiss the charges against Paul from the beginning. Now he is desperate to save face. Meanwhile, Paul is yet again in front of powerful leaders with no immediate prospect of release. God is not obviously present in this almost absurd scene where kings and other high-ranking officials are gathered to write something to keep Festus in office rather than ensure justice for Paul.

Psalms can be particularly helpful when facing seemingly hopeless situations and Paul would have known many by heart. Perhaps he took comfort from Psalm 37, reminding him and us that God is aware of our circumstances and, even if our enemies triumph for a while, God will overcome. Our task is to wait patiently and trust in the Lord.

Prayer
Read and pray slowly through Psalm 37, particularly verses 3–9.

LAKSHMI JEFFRIES

Beyond religion

Agrippa said to Paul, 'You have permission to speak for yourself.' So Paul motioned with his hand and began his defence: 'King Agrippa, I consider myself fortunate to stand before you today as I make my defence against all the accusations of the Jews, and especially so because you are well acquainted with all the Jewish customs and controversies. Therefore, I beg you to listen to me patiently. The Jewish people all know the way I have lived ever since I was a child... and can testify... that I conformed to the strictest sect of our religion, living as a Pharisee. And now it is because of my hope in what God has promised our ancestors that I am on trial today. This is the promise our twelve tribes are hoping to see fulfilled... King Agrippa, it is because of this hope that these Jews are accusing me. Why should any of you consider it incredible that God raises the dead?

Paul makes his longest speech in the book of Acts and makes it primarily to Agrippa and those who share a common understanding of the Jewish faith. Having been led by the Holy Spirit to preach the good news of Jesus to the Gentiles, Paul is now inspired to speak to those he formerly represented, some of whom have known him since childhood.

When someone chooses to follow Jesus, they see life through new eyes. Paul held a set of beliefs very strictly and says that he now has the same beliefs, especially in the resurrection of the dead, but is no longer a Pharisee. To Paul it is absurd that he should be on trial for what he holds in common with his erstwhile fellow believers.

It can be hard to speak about Jesus to those whose customs we once shared. There can be a feeling of betrayal now that we see things differently. Like Paul, as we pray and encounter Jesus daily, we discover points of contact between our ways and those of others and can use these to share the gospel. We need the inspiration of the Holy Spirit to remain respectful yet distinctive.

Prayer
Lord, show me as a Christian what I have in common with others.

LAKSHMI JEFFRIES

ACTS 26:9–14 (NIV, ABRIDGED)

Then and now

'I too was convinced that I ought to do all that was possible to oppose the name of Jesus of Nazareth... On the authority of the chief priests I put many of the Lord's people in prison, and when they were put to death, I cast my vote against them. Many a time I went from one synagogue to another to have them punished, and I tried to force them to blaspheme. I was so obsessed with persecuting them that I even hunted them down in foreign cities. On one of these journeys I was going to Damascus with the authority and commission of the chief priests. About noon, King Agrippa, as I was on the road, I saw a light from heaven, brighter than the sun, blazing around me and my companions. We all fell to the ground, and I heard a voice saying to me in Aramaic, "Saul, Saul, why do you persecute me? It is hard for you to kick against the goads."'

The contrast between Paul's former life and current faith is crystal clear. Paul had seen it as his duty to eliminate those who did anything in the name of Jesus or to force them to renounce him. He persecuted Christians with the authority and blessing of his religious leaders. The tragedy is that he sincerely believed he was acting according to God's will. There would be no doubt in Agrippa's mind that Paul was zealous for God among his people. Then came the voice through the light: Paul was, in fact, persecuting God himself!

It is essential to keep listening to God through prayer and scripture, alongside other Christians, to avoid the possibility that our well-intentioned actions will have disastrous consequences. So many of us say a quick prayer at the beginning or end of an activity and assume we have been faithful to God. Recently I was with a group of Christians planning a course of action that we agreed was good, until someone challenged us and we discovered, having stopped to pray, that our ideas were not necessarily the best in God's eyes. Our focus had been on immediate need and, like Paul, we had instead to focus on God himself.

Prayer
Loving God, help me to discern your will.

LAKSHMI JEFFRIES

Darkness to light

'"I am Jesus, whom you are persecuting," the Lord replied. "… I have appeared to you to appoint you as a servant and as a witness of what you have seen and will see of me. I will rescue you from your own people and from the Gentiles. I am sending you to them to open their eyes and turn them from darkness to light… so that they may receive forgiveness of sins and a place among those who are sanctified by faith in me." So then, King Agrippa, I was not disobedient to the vision from heaven… I preached that they should repent and turn to God and demonstrate their repentance by their deeds… God has helped me to this very day; so I stand here and testify to small and great alike… that the Messiah would suffer and, as the first to rise from the dead, would bring the message of light to his own people and to the Gentiles.'

The movement from darkness to light is a significant metaphor for God's salvation throughout the Bible. Agrippa and others who had studied Isaiah would remember Isaiah 42:6–7, where God calls the prophet as a light to the Gentiles and to open the eyes of the blind. Although Paul does not refer to his own temporary physical blindness, he knows that God restored his sight and has continued to help Paul to be faithful to his calling.

'There's none so blind as those who will not see' is a familiar proverb, speaking of how people can choose to ignore something they prefer not to acknowledge. Paul shows clearly that Jesus is God's promised Messiah who suffered and was raised from death to bring the message of light. Unfortunately, Paul himself is on trial because of the lack of recognition of Jesus by his former leaders. Still today there are many who choose not to see Jesus for who he is, ignoring the prompting of God's Holy Spirit to move from darkness to light. All we can do is, in word and action, to share our stories of life with Jesus and continue to pray for those we love.

Prayer
Pray for people you know who currently choose not to see Jesus.

LAKSHMI JEFFRIES

What do you think?

At this point Festus interrupted Paul's defence. 'You are out of your mind, Paul!' he shouted. 'Your great learning is driving you insane.' 'I am not insane, most excellent Festus,' Paul replied. 'What I am saying is true and reasonable. The king is familiar with these things, and I can speak freely to him. I am convinced that none of this has escaped his notice, because it was not done in a corner. King Agrippa, do you believe the prophets? I know you do.'

Festus suggests that Paul has 'lost the plot'! Festus is a sensible Roman leader who will not countenance any ridiculous notions for which there are no logical explanations. Paul remains respectful and suggests that all he has said makes complete sense. He is addressing his remarks to Agrippa, though, who, due to his existing religious beliefs, is already familiar with much of the background to Paul's story. So Paul politely returns to the king to confirm this in two ways: first, Christians in general and Paul in particular live out their faith in public rather than having philosophical discussions tucked away from public scrutiny. Agrippa will have seen Christians in action and can vouch for the validity of Paul's statements. The second confirmation for Paul comes from a direct question: does King Agrippa believe the prophets? Thankfully for the king, Paul answers his own question. Had Agrippa said 'No', he would have significantly undermined his position as a religious leader. If, however, he'd admitted that he believed the prophets, the king would have had to explain why he did not see Jesus as the Messiah.

Christian faith is not a set of ideas to which adherents give intellectual assent; nor is it a set of rules about behaviour. Instead, Christians are those who follow Jesus, whom we know by faith in God through the Holy Spirit. Festus struggles with the intellectual side of faith: if he cannot see something, it cannot be real. Meanwhile, Agrippa is used to a code of conduct so that he knows exactly what God expects him to do, but battles with the notion of encountering God by the Holy Spirit.

Reflection

Through his disciples living out his good news, Jesus continues to confound the world.

LAKSHMI JEFFRIES

The end of this chapter

Then Agrippa said to Paul, 'Do you think that in such a short time you can persuade me to be a Christian?' Paul replied, 'Short time or long—I pray to God that not only you but all who are listening to me today may become what I am, except for these chains.' The king rose, and with him the governor and Bernice and those sitting with them. After they left the room, they began saying to one another, 'This man is not doing anything that deserves death or imprisonment.' Agrippa said to Festus, 'This man could have been set free if he had not appealed to Caesar.'

Agrippa does not want to hear any more, perhaps because he finds Paul's argument persuasive and fears that, in time, he might become a Christian! Paul is passionate: however long it takes, he wants everyone present to follow Jesus as he does, although in freedom rather than under arrest. Meanwhile, he has convinced Agrippa and the other officials that he is not guilty of misconduct under either Roman or Jewish law.

At every stage in the proceedings Paul has shown respect to those he has addressed. At the same time, he has courageously told his story and been open about his desire to bring his hearers to faith in Jesus. He must now go to Rome without anyone having been converted as a result of these encounters.

Katy was the only Christian in her workplace. She got on well with others and, although she longed for opportunities to speak about her faith, they never came. She chose instead to pray for her colleagues and enjoy developing friendships with them. After a number of years, Katy was transferred to another part of the country. A few days before she was due to leave, one of the others invited her to meet his family and talk about why she believed in God. He had been impressed by her attitude over the years and now felt able to ask questions. There were no dramatic conversions, but, a decade later, Katy heard that the whole family had come to Christian faith and were active members of their local church.

Reflection
*Jesus promised that the Holy Spirit would teach us what to say
(Luke 12:11–12).*

LAKSHMI JEFFRIES

Supporting Barnabas in Schools
with a gift in your will

For many charities, income from legacies is crucial and represents a significant aspect of their funding each year. Legacies enable charities to plan ahead and often provide the funding to develop new projects. Legacies make a significant difference to the ability of charities to achieve their purpose. In just this way, a legacy to support BRF's ministry would make a huge difference.

Take our Barnabas in Schools ministry, for example. In our increasingly secular society, fewer and fewer children are growing up with any real knowledge or understanding of the Bible or the Christian faith. We're passionate about enabling children and their teachers in primary schools to explore Christianity creatively, and to learn both about and from the Bible, within RE and Collective Worship.

Our Barnabas RE Days, using storytelling, mime and drama, are in great demand. They explore big themes (Who am I? Whose world? Who is my neighbour? It's not fair!) along with the major Christian festivals. We also offer specialist In-Service Training (INSET) sessions for teachers, along with a wide range of publications and a website with information, articles and downloadable resources.

Since 2011 we have introduced a brand new theme for each new academic year, with a Barnabas RE Day, INSET session, classroom resource and support materials on the web. We've encouraged many schools to take a fresh look at the Bible; we've helped them explore, through the eyes of faith and belief, values linked to the Olympic and Paralympic Games in London; most recently we've enabled them to explore Christianity as a worldwide faith. Our new theme for 2013–2014 invites them to explore the Christian themes and imagery in C.S. Lewis's 'Chronicles of Narnia' series.

A legacy gift could help fund the development of future themes for Barnabas in Schools.

Throughout its history, BRF's ministry has been enabled thanks to the generosity of those who have shared its vision and supported its work both by giving during their lifetime and also through legacy gifts. We hope you may consider a legacy gift to help us continue to take this work forward in the decades to come.

If you would like more information about making a gift to BRF in your will or to discuss how a specific bequest could be used to develop our ministry, please email enquiries@brf.org.uk or phone 01865 319700.

This page is deliberately left blank.

The BRF

Magazine

An interview with Tony Sharp

In 2012, BRF brought Who Let The Dads Out? into its family of core ministries at the invitation of Hoole Baptist Church, Chester, where it all began. Tony Sharp is BRF's National Coordinator for this ministry.

Tony, tell us about yourself.

The first thing to say is that I'm a dad! I have one delightful daughter, called Laura, who is 18 and in her final year of Sixth Form. She is hoping to study Ecology and Environmental Biology, and at the moment has got us on a two-month 'fish fast' to help raise our awareness of the threat to our marine ecology. I'm really missing my Friday fish suppers, though! I'm also happily married to the lovely Brenda; we met at Brighton Road Baptist Church in Horsham, Sussex, got to know each other by sharing a commute to London, and have now been married for 24 years. When we married we moved to Newport Pagnell, and then moved again to Chester in 1997. I'm a mechanical engineer by training and have mostly worked (and continue to do so) in the water industry. We worship at Hoole Baptist Church in Chester, which is how I come to be so involved in Who Let The Dads Out?

My other great pleasure is sport, my favourites being tennis, football and my latest passion, golf, which brings an altogether different type of challenge.

So what is Who Let The Dads Out?

Who Let The Dads Out? is an umbrella name for a number of ideas that can help churches to engage with fathers and male carers in their local communities. The initial, or 'gateway', idea is for churches to set up and run a Who Let The Dads Out? toddler group that typically runs once a month for two hours on a Saturday morning. It provides a relaxed welcome, including tea, coffee and bacon butties (or similar) for the dads, juice and biscuits for the children, the usual church toddler group activities, and space for good conversations.

These groups meet a real social need and provide natural opportunities to explore faith issues within the group setting and/or through related follow-on activities that we have also developed under the Who Let The Dads Out? umbrella.

Why does it make a difference?

Dads and male carers need opportunities to spend time with their children—at all ages, but particularly when the children are very young. We need men to engage in their role as parents for the benefit of the child, the family unit and the local community. There are many statistics to demonstrate that children with an engaged father or male carer do better at school and in later life.

We also know that men are leaving the church but that, conversely, when a man comes to faith, the chances of this influencing the faith of the rest of the family are high.

What are you busy with right now?

My two core responsibilities are to let churches know about the initiative and encourage them to consider if it is right for their context, and to provide support to the leaders of the existing groups. This includes running workshops in different regions, establishing social media networks and keeping them active, writing the quarterly newsletter, developing resources for groups, organising conferences and helping to develop a new website. Right now, I'm also putting a trial in place for regional reps (similar to Messy Church Regional Coordinators), and writing, along with Mark Chester, a new Who Let The Dads Out? resource. It's also important that I have input into our funding strategy, because we need to raise £50,000 every year for the next three years to make our plans happen.

Are there things your own dad taught you?

My father died just over two years ago, and of course I miss him greatly. He worked all his life as an actuary and part of his legacy has been to give my mum, my brother and me a secure financial base.

I have him to thank for my love of sport and my appreciation for sporting endeavour—the realisation that taking part and competing are more important than winning. As a rule, I try to be humble in victory and gracious in defeat. In particular, I remember the fact that my dad taught me to swim. It was only much later that I learnt how unenthusiastic he was about swimming and, therefore, the extent to which he was going out of his comfort zone in order to teach me.

I know that I was unconditionally loved and accepted by both my parents. I was never pressurised to follow a particular career path or to be 'successful'; I was given loving guidance and support and encouraged to find my way in life. I hope their modelling of this attitude has taught me to adopt a similar approach with Laura.

Hearing the call

Naomi Starkey

It was there for years, niggling away in the background—that sense of 'something more'. What was it? I loved my work in publishing, first at SPCK and (since 1997) at BRF, and certainly when one or two people (as they have since reminded me) suggested that I might have a call to ordained ministry, my response was, 'Don't be ridiculous!' I have been a vicar's daughter and a vicar's sister, and am still a vicar's wife. Ordination to the priesthood was what other people did, not me.

From time to time in my regular staff review, I discussed ideas such as training for Reader ministry or doing some sort of theology degree. Nothing ever seemed quite to fit and the timing never seemed right, either. Then a whole lot of 'coincidences' came together—and now here I am juggling my BRF work with part-time training for ordination to 'non-stipendiary' or 'self-supporting' ministry. In other words, I don't give up the day job but will (all being well) end up as a priest in the Church in Wales, able to celebrate the Eucharist, preach, do pastoral care and so on. If working as a tent-maker as well as an apostle was good enough for St Paul, then combining the roles of an NSM/SSM and commissioning editor is good enough for me!

Why wasn't my well-established 'ministry of publishing' enough? After all, as editor of *New Daylight* I am responsible for producing devotional material that nurtures the faith of tens of thousands of readers. It is an amazing privilege and huge responsibility—and I continue to enjoy it—but over time I have realised that, as well as editing books and Bible reading notes, I want to be 'at the coal face', working with others to help connect people with God's transformative love. I have occasionally led quiet days and given talks on a variety of topics, but what I long for is a regular relationship with a local church or group of churches, helping them grow as Christian disciples.

Probably the main factor in crystallising my call was moving to Wales in 2011. After years of urban living, latterly in a challenging city centre environment, I was able to re-engage with small rural communities and small rural churches, and remembered how much I loved them and felt at home among them. Country life has changed significantly since the late 1980s when I last lived in such a context, not least because the internet now connects even remote villages (if the broadband connection behaves itself), but the strong family networks, deep roots and sense of continuity still contrast with much that characterises present-day cities, in my experience, anyway.

In practical terms, my part-time training is run through the St Seiriol Centre of Bangor Diocese (named after the sixth-century Welsh saint who founded a monastery at Penmon, across the Menai Straits from Bangor). Each week I meet with a group in a nearby village to study the diocesan *Exploring Faith* theology course, which involves discussing the term's set book, doing four pieces of assessed written work and attending a termly Saturday school. While fitting in the necessary course reading is sometimes difficult, it has also proved fascinating and of real benefit to my ongoing publishing work.

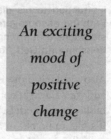

An exciting mood of positive change

I have greatly enjoyed a placement in a group of local churches, although in mid-Wales 'local' can still mean a round trip of over 30 miles! After two decades or so as a clergy wife, involved in aspects of church life from leading intercessions to running the Sunday school (although I have never yet made it as far as the flower rota), I was surprised to find how different it felt being up at the front, wearing robes, and being responsible for leading the service as a whole. I have had the chance to reflect on the daunting responsibility of conducting funerals, especially when a death has occurred in tragic circumstances, and I have discovered how a full and joyful time of worship can be had with a congregation of just six. Small really can be beautiful.

Rural churches face many challenges, but in the Bangor diocese I feel there is an exciting mood of positive change and a 'can do' attitude, in the wake of the groundbreaking Harries Report. This recommended, among other things, a move towards appointing clergy to 'Ministry Areas', clusters of parishes along the lines of secondary school catchment areas, thus increasing opportunities to share plans, resources and mutual encouragement. The move involves a dramatically enhanced role for the laity as well as a lot of scope for NSM/SSM clergy—which is how I hope to be involved, after my ordination, first to the diaconate in June 2014, and, the following year, to the priesthood.

Recommended reading

Kevin Ball

If you are one of the many BRF daily notes readers who enjoy supplementing your reading during Lent with the BRF Lent book, make sure you get your copy of *Welcoming the Way of the Cross*. Retreat leader Barbara Mosse focuses on Jesus' instruction to his disciples to take up their cross and follow him. With the encouragement of scripture, Barbara explores some of the situations that prompt us to seek a deeper and more authentic relationship with God. You can read a short extract on pages 148–149.

Also available now is the new book from popular author, broadcaster and *New Daylight* contributor David Winter, *At the End of the Day*. Using biblical role models, David takes you on a wry, humorous look at what it's like to be old in an era of the relentlessly new.

Following the wide success of her first book, *Growing a Caring Church*, Wendy Billington's new book, *I'm Fine*, is for anyone with a passion for helping people who are encountering difficulties in life—difficulties that are often hidden behind the response 'I'm fine'. Wendy offers practical advice from many years of pastoral experience to help you bring support and encouragement.

A new writer for BRF is Daniel Muñoz, whose book *Transformed by the Beloved* focuses on the spirituality of St John of the Cross. Daniel helpfully explains John's use of the 'night' metaphor in spiritual formation and helps us to appreciate the beauty and power of his poetry.

Finally, if you need some light distraction, Jeremy Fletcher's humorous, one-line reflections from church ministry, *Rules for Reverends* just might be the ideal option:

'If the whole team is last-minute, you'll get on well with each other and your church will learn what faith is all about.'

Enjoy!

Transformed by the Beloved
A guide to spiritual formation with St John of the Cross
Daniel Muñoz

An introduction to the spirituality and poetry of John of the Cross, the radical Spanish mystic. This book can be read in two ways—either as an introduction to the key themes and spiritual teachings of John of the Cross or as a guide to spiritual formation that can be used by individuals or a small group. At the end of each chapter, there are questions for prayer and reflection, often with reference to John's poems. Most of John's poems can be found at the end of the book, with the author's own English translations alongside.

Daniel Muñoz is an Anglican priest and theologian. He has led art and spirituality projects in parish churches in the Oxford Diocese, where he served as a priest for nine years, and is founder of the Marlow Art and Spirituality Network. He has a personal interest in 16th-century Spanish mysticism, especially the life and works of John of the Cross, Celtic spirituality and Christian art.

pb, 978 1 84101 584 2, £6.99

Rules for Reverends
Jeremy Fletcher

A fun but, at the same time, insightful collection of around 250 'rules' for life in church ministry, ranging from straightforwardly humorous observations to shrewd and pithy one-liners that will make you pause for thought. Divided into 20 sections, ranging from Christmas to 'What (not) to wear', the book is illustrated by *Church Times* cartoonist Dave Walker, whose offbeat style perfectly complements the author's laconic approach, honed through years of ministry and sitting on church committees as well as General Synod!

Jeremy Fletcher is Vicar of Beverley Minster, Yorkshire, having spent seven years as Canon Precentor at York Minster. A member of the General Synod, he is an enthusiastic blogger and Tweeter, as well as serving on the Church of England's Liturgical Commission, involved in the development of Common Worship.

pb, 978 1 84101 657 3, 128 pages, £6.99

I'm Fine
Removing masks and growing into wholeness
Wendy Billington

A down-to-earth and sensitive exploration of a number of difficult pastoral issues that crop up in local church life, from the emotional to the material, including loneliness, financial difficulties, low self-esteem, depression, marriage problems, desertion, dementia, alcohol misuse, domestic abuse, pornography and loss of faith. Such issues are all too often hidden behind a bright smile and the response 'I'm fine!' but can derail faith and devastate individuals, families and the church community if they are not addressed properly.

Drawing on her experience as a counsellor and church pastoral worker, as well as her own life experiences, the author sensitively explores the issues through case studies, showing the challenges of helping those who face such issues and suggesting practical ways forward.

Wendy Billington coordinates the pastoral care programme at a large Anglican parish church in Kent, south-east England. Her work includes providing training in pastoral skills, listening to people's concerns, bereavement care, marriage enrichment and supporting cancer sufferers and their families. She is a director of the Sevenoaks Christian Counselling Service and has also written Growing a Caring Church *(BRF, 2010).*

pb, 978 1 84101 871 3, 144 pages, £6.99

At the End of the Day
Enjoying life in the departure lounge
David Winter

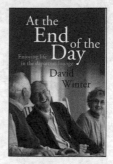

An octogenarian takes a wryly humorous look at what it's like to be old in an era of the relentlessly new. Turning to the Bible, David Winter explores its store of timeless wisdom, encouragement and reassurance about what it has always meant to grow old and be old. The book is structured around a series of fascinating biblical pictures, from the legendary Methuselah to the feisty Sarah and the great leader Moses, from the picture of inevitable decline as the Preacher saw it in Ecclesiastes to the glorious Nunc Dimittis of old Simeon in the temple.

'At the end of the day' is a well-worn phrase, yet looking at life as if it were a single day, with dawn, noon, sunny afternoon, twilight and then darkness and sleep, provides a sort of contracted chronology of a journey we are all taking. Those who are at, or beyond, tea-time (as well as their friends and family members) may find that this book offers an essentially optimistic, positive and attractive picture of both the present and the future.

David Winter is one of the UK's most popular and long-established Christian writers and broadcasters. He has written many books over the last 60 years and is a regular contributor to New Daylight.

pb, 978 0 85746 057 8, 128 pages, £6.99

To order copies of any of these books, please turn to the order form on page 155, or visit www.brfonline.org.uk.

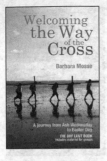

An extract from *Welcoming the Way of the Cross*

In today's fast-paced culture, people crave space for rest and renewal, for restoration of both body and soul. *Welcoming the Way of the Cross* explores how creating this space can be a part of Lenten discipline and be understood as 'hospitality' in its broadest sense—making space to be open to God, to ourselves and to each other. This short extract is taken from the readings for Week 5, entitled 'Open to the world'. It is based on a reading from Acts 11:1–18, in which the apostle Peter explains his vision of the unclean animals and the subsequent gift of the Holy Spirit to the Gentile Cornelius and his household.

We began our journey this Lent a long way from home, in the company of the prodigal son in 'a distant country', and of Jacob, who cheated his twin Esau out of his birthright and their father Isaac's blessing. From those places of alienation and isolation, we began to catch glimpses of a wonderful and mysterious truth—that the loving God who formed us in the womb (Psalm 139) seeks to draw us, in spite of our sin and from however far we may have travelled, back into the warmth of his loving embrace…

As our spiritual journey deepens, we are faced with the same kind of challenge that faced the early Christians—to resist the ever-present temptation to put God into a box, attempting to confine him to a place in our thinking and lives that gives us the illusion of security and safety. We tend to prefer to stay with what we know, but God constantly challenges us to allow him to stretch and transcend our boundaries. As the American poet Minnie Louise Haskins expressed it, 'Step out into the darkness and put your hand into the hand of God. That shall be to you better than light, and safer than a known way.'

As we consider Peter's vision concerning the 'clean' and 'unclean' animals, we join the narrative at a point where the fledgling Christian church is being coaxed into taking a quantum leap forward in its understanding of the ways of God. Proud of their heritage and conscious of their destiny as God's chosen people, the idea that God was using the believers as a channel of his love to the Gentiles was deeply unsettling, despite the hints embedded in Israel's own history (see Genesis 17:4–7; Joshua 5:13–14; Isaiah 52:10; Luke 2:29–32).

Something of the disciples' confusion and uncertainty is reflected in the opening verses of Acts 11. To the consternation of many, it was becoming clear that the gift of the Holy Spirit was not reserved for 'circumcised believers' alone, but that Gentiles also (of whom Cornelius the centurion has already been introduced as a shining example, in Acts 10:1–8) were being equally blessed. Even Peter, despite living and working so closely with Jesus, was resistant to this development, and yet his cooperation in this venture was vital. As the American theologian Robert W. Wall bluntly expresses it, 'God's redemptive purposes for Gentiles could not be realised unless the apostle changed his mind.' Peter, in this passage, is facing the suspicion and accusations of his fellow believers as he explains to them that the triple repetition within his vision finally jolted his understanding to a new level.

The difficulty that Peter and his fellow believers experienced may be a familiar one. The fact that we know we are special to God and are deeply loved by him is a wonderful gift, but it carries with it the danger that we may come to view ourselves as somehow more special, or more privileged, than others. Robert W. Wall writes, 'Those believers who think themselves among God's "elect" are often inclined on this theological basis to think that God has not chosen anyone else who disagrees with their beliefs and customs.' We have seen the global fall-out from this thinking, throughout history and down to the present day—from Crusades, burning in the name of religion, the unimaginable evil of the holocaust and ethnic cleansings the world over, to the horrors of 9/11. But fear of the unknown also constrains and restricts us far more immediately—from our reactions to those whom we perceive as 'outsiders' in our communities to the endless bickering and defensiveness clustering around whatever are the current disagreements within our churches. We have a long way to go before we can confidently say with Peter; 'I truly understand that God shows no partiality, but in every nation anyone who fears him and does what is right is acceptable to him' (Acts 10:34–35).

A question
'I truly understand that God shows no partiality' (Acts 10:34). To what extent is this true in the life of your own church?

To order a copy of this book, please turn to the order form on page 155, or visit www.brfonline.org.uk.

As a Christian charity, BRF is involved in seven distinct yet complementary areas.

- **BRF** (www.brf.org.uk) resources adults for their spiritual journey through Bible reading notes, books and Quiet Days. BRF also provides the infrastructure that supports our other specialist ministries.
- **Foundations21** (www.foundations21.net) provides flexible and innovative ways for individuals and groups to explore their Christian faith and discipleship through a multimedia internet-based resource.
- **Messy Church** (www.messychurch.org.uk), led by Lucy Moore, enables churches all over the UK (and increasingly abroad) to reach children and adults beyond the fringes of the church.
- **Barnabas in Churches** (www.barnabasinchurches.org.uk) helps churches to support, resource and develop their children's ministry with the under-11s more effectively .
- **Barnabas in Schools** (www.barnabasinschools.org.uk) enables primary school children and teachers to explore Christianity creatively and bring the Bible alive within RE and Collective Worship.
- **Faith in Homes** (www.faithinhomes.org.uk) supports families to explore and live out the Christian faith at home.
- **Who Let The Dads Out** (www.wholetthedadsout.org) inspires churches to engage with dads and their pre-school children.

At the heart of BRF's ministry is a desire to equip adults and children for Christian living—helping them to read and understand the Bible, explore prayer and grow as disciples of Jesus. We need your help to make an impact on the local church, local schools and the wider community.

- You could support BRF's ministry with a one-off gift or regular donation (using the response form on page 153).
- You could consider making a bequest to BRF in your will.
- You could encourage your church to support BRF as part of your church's giving to home mission—perhaps focusing on a specific area of our ministry, or a particular member of our Barnabas team.
- Most important of all, you could support BRF with your prayers.

If you would like to discuss how a specific gift or bequest could be used in the development of our ministry, please phone 01865 319700 or email enquiries@brf.org.uk.

Whatever you can do or give, we thank you for your support.

Thank you for reading BRF Bible reading notes. BRF has been producing a variety of Bible reading notes for over 90 years, helping people all over the UK and the world connect with the Bible on a personal level every day.

Could you help us find other people who would enjoy our notes?

We produce a Bible Reading Resource Pack for church groups to use to encourage regular Bible reading.

This FREE pack contains:

- Samples of all BRF Bible reading notes.
- Our Resources for Personal Bible Reading catalogue, providing all you need to know about our Bible reading notes.
- A ready-to-use church magazine feature about BRF notes.
- Ready-made sermon and all-age service ideas to help your church into the Bible (ideal for Bible Sunday events).
- And much more!

How to order your FREE pack:

- Visit: www.biblereadingnotes.org.uk/request-a-bible-reading-resources-pack/
- Telephone: 01865 319700 between 9.15 and 17.30
- Post: Complete the form below and post to: Bible Reading Resource Pack, BRF, 15 The Chambers, Vineyard, Abingdon, OX14 3FE

Name _____

Address _____

_____

_____ Postcode _____

Telephone _____

Email _____

Please send me _____ Bible Reading Resources Pack(s)

This pack is produced free of charge for all UK addresses but, if you wish to offer a donation towards our costs, this would be appreciated. If you require a pack to be sent outside of the UK, please contact us for details of postage and packing charges. Tel: +44 1865 319700. Thank you.

BRF is a Registered Charity

NEW DAYLIGHT SUBSCRIPTIONS

Please note our subscription rates 2014–2015. From the May 2014 issue, the new subscription rates will be:

Individual subscriptions covering 3 issues for under 5 copies, payable in advance (including postage and packing):

	UK	SURFACE	AIRMAIL
NEW DAYLIGHT each set of 3 p.a.	£15.99	£23.25	£25.50
NEW DAYLIGHT 3-year sub i.e. 9 issues	£40.50	N/A	N/A
(Not available for Deluxe)			
NEW DAYLIGHT DELUXE each set of 3 p.a.	£19.80	£30.75	£36.75

Group subscriptions covering 3 issues for 5 copies or more, sent to ONE UK address (post free).

NEW DAYLIGHT	£12.75	each set of 3 p.a.
NEW DAYLIGHT DELUXE	£15.75	each set of 3 p.a.

Overseas group subscription rates available on request.
Contact enquiries@brf.org.uk.

Please note that the annual billing period for Group Subscriptions runs from 1 May to 30 April.

Copies of the notes may also be obtained from Christian bookshops:

NEW DAYLIGHT	£4.25 each copy
NEW DAYLIGHT DELUXE	£5.25 each copy

Visit www.biblereadingnotes.org.uk for information about our other Bible reading notes and Apple apps for iPhone and iPod touch.

BRF MINISTRY APPEAL RESPONSE FORM

I want to help BRF by funding some of its core ministries. Please use my gift for:

❏ Where most needed ❏ Barnabas Children's Ministry ❏ Foundations21
❏ Messy Church ❏ Who Let The Dads Out?

Please complete all relevant sections of this form and print clearly.

Title _____ First name/initials _____ Surname _____

Address _____

_____ Postcode _____

Telephone _____ Email _____

Regular giving

If you would like to give by standing order, please contact Debra McKnight (tel: 01235 462305; email debra.mcknight@brf.org.uk; write to BRF address).

If you would like to give by direct debit, please tick the box below and fill in details:

❏ I would like to make a regular gift of £ _____ per month / quarter / year
(delete as appropriate) by Direct Debit. (Please complete the form on page 159.)

One-off donation

Please accept my special gift of
❏ £10 ❏ £50 ❏ £100 (other) £ _____ by

❏ Cheque / Charity Voucher payable to 'BRF'
❏ Visa / Mastercard / Charity Card
(delete as appropriate)

Name on card _____

Card no. [ ][ ][ ][ ] [ ][ ][ ][ ] [ ][ ][ ][ ] [ ][ ][ ][ ]

Start date [ ][ ][ ]   Expiry date [ ][ ][ ]

Security code [ ][ ][ ]

Signature _____ Date _____

❏ I would like to give a legacy to BRF. Please send me further information.

If you would like to Gift Aid your donation, please fill in the form overleaf.

Please detach and send this completed form to: Debra McKnight, BRF,
15 The Chambers, Vineyard, Abingdon OX14 3FE.   BRF is a Registered Charity (No.233280)

GIFT AID DECLARATION

Bible Reading Fellowship

Please treat as Gift Aid donations all qualifying gifts of money made
today ☐   in the past 4 years ☐   in the future ☐   (tick all that apply)

I confirm I have paid or will pay an amount of Income Tax and/or Capital Gains Tax for each tax year (6 April to 5 April) that is at least equal to the amount of tax that all the charities that I donate to will reclaim on my gifts for that tax year. I understand that other taxes such as VAT or Council Tax do not qualify. I understand the charity will reclaim 28p of tax on every £1 that I gave up to 5 April 2008 and will reclaim 25p of tax on every £1 that I give on or after 6 April 2008.

Donor's details

Title _____ First name or initials _____ Surname _____

Full home address _____

_____

Postcode _____

Date _____

Signature _____

Please notify Bible Reading Fellowship if you:
* want to cancel this declaration
* change your name or home address
* no longer pay sufficient tax on your income and/or capital gains.

If you pay Income Tax at the higher or additional rate and want to receive the additional tax relief due to you, you must include all your Gift Aid donations on your Self-Assessment tax return or ask HM Revenue and Customs to adjust your tax code.

ND0114

BRF PUBLICATIONS ORDER FORM

Please send me the following book(s):	Quantity	Price	Total
180 3 Welcoming the Way of the Cross (B. Mosse)	_____	£7.99	_____
584 2 Transformed by the Beloved (D. Muñoz)	_____	£6.99	_____
057 8 At the End of the Day (D. Winter)	_____	£6.99	_____
657 3 Rules for Reverends (J. Fletcher)	_____	£6.99	_____
871 3 I'm Fine (W. Billington)	_____	£6.99	_____
885 0 Who Let The Dads Out? (M. Chester)	_____	£6.99	_____

Total cost of books £ _____

Donation £ _____

Postage and packing £ _____

TOTAL £ _____

POSTAGE AND PACKING CHARGES				
order value	UK	Europe	Surface	Air Mail
£7.00 & under	£1.25	£3.00	£3.50	£5.50
£7.01–£30.00	£2.25	£5.50	£6.50	£10.00
Over £30.00	free	prices on request		

Please complete the payment details below and send with payment to: **BRF, 15 The Chambers, Vineyard, Abingdon OX14 3FE**

Name _____

Address _____

_____ Postcode _____

Tel _____ Email _____

Total enclosed £ _____ (cheques should be made payable to 'BRF')

Please charge my Visa ❏ Mastercard ❏ Switch card ❏ with £ _____

Card no: ☐☐☐☐☐☐☐☐☐☐☐☐☐☐☐☐☐☐

Expires ☐☐☐☐   Security code ☐☐☐

Issue no (Switch only) ☐☐☐☐

Signature (essential if paying by credit/Switch) _____

NEW DAYLIGHT INDIVIDUAL SUBSCRIPTIONS

❏ I would like to take out a subscription myself:

Your name _____

Your address _____

_____ Postcode _____

Tel _____ Email _____

Please send *New Daylight* beginning with the May 2014 / September 2014 /
January 2015 issue: (delete as applicable)

(please tick box)	UK	SURFACE	AIR MAIL
NEW DAYLIGHT	❏ £15.99	❏ £23.25	❏ £25.50
NEW DAYLIGHT 3-year sub	❏ £40.50		
NEW DAYLIGHT DELUXE	❏ £19.80	❏ £30.75	❏ £36.75
NEW DAYLIGHT daily email only	❏ £12.75 (UK and overseas)		

Please complete the payment details below and send with appropriate
payment to: **BRF, 15 The Chambers, Vineyard, Abingdon OX14 3FE**

Total enclosed £ _____ (cheques should be made payable to 'BRF')

Please charge my Visa ❏ Mastercard ❏ Switch card ❏ with £ _____

Card no: ☐☐☐☐ ☐☐☐☐ ☐☐☐☐ ☐☐☐☐ ☐☐☐☐

Expires ☐☐☐☐ Security code ☐☐☐

Issue no (Switch only) ☐☐☐☐

Signature (essential if paying by card) _____

To set up a direct debit, please also complete the form on page 159 and send
it to BRF with this form.

NEW DAYLIGHT GIFT SUBSCRIPTIONS

❏ I would like to give a gift subscription (please provide both names and addresses:

Your name _____

Your address _____

_____ Postcode _____

Tel _____ Email _____

Gift subscription name _____

Gift subscription address _____

_____ Postcode _____

Gift message (20 words max. or include your own gift card for the recipient)

_____

_____

Please send *New Daylight* beginning with the May 2014 / September 2014 / January 2015 issue: (delete as applicable)

(please tick box)	UK	SURFACE	AIR MAIL
NEW DAYLIGHT	❏ £15.99	❏ £23.25	❏ £25.50
NEW DAYLIGHT 3-year sub	❏ £40.50		
NEW DAYLIGHT DELUXE	❏ £19.80	❏ £30.75	❏ £36.75
NEW DAYLIGHT daily email only	❏ £12.75 (UK and overseas)		

Please complete the payment details below and send with appropriate payment to: **BRF, 15 The Chambers, Vineyard, Abingdon OX14 3FE**

Total enclosed £ _____ (cheques should be made payable to 'BRF')

Please charge my Visa ❏ Mastercard ❏ Switch card ❏ with £ _____

Card no: ☐☐☐☐ ☐☐☐☐ ☐☐☐☐ ☐☐☐☐ ☐☐☐☐

Expires ☐☐☐☐ **Security code** ☐☐☐

Issue no (Switch only) ☐☐☐☐

Signature (essential if paying by card) _____

To set up a direct debit, please also complete the form on page 159 and send it to BRF with this form.

Now you can pay for your annual subscription to BRF notes using Direct Debit. You need only give your bank details once, and the payment is made automatically every year until you cancel it. If you would like to pay by Direct Debit, please use the form opposite, entering your BRF account number under 'Reference'.

You are fully covered by the Direct Debit Guarantee:

The Direct Debit Guarantee

- This Guarantee is offered by all banks and building societies that accept instructions to pay Direct Debits.
- If there are any changes to the amount, date or frequency of your Direct Debit, The Bible Reading Fellowship will notify you 10 working days in advance of your account being debited or as otherwise agreed. If you request The Bible Reading Fellowship to collect a payment, confirmation of the amount and date will be given to you at the time of the request.
- If an error is made in the payment of your Direct Debit, by The Bible Reading Fellowship or your bank or building society, you are entitled to a full and immediate refund of the amount paid from your bank or building society.
  - – If you receive a refund you are not entitled to, you must pay it back when The Bible Reading Fellowship asks you to.
- You can cancel a Direct Debit at any time by simply contacting your bank or building society. Written confirmation may be required. Please also notify us.

The Bible Reading Fellowship

Instruction to your bank or
building society to pay by Direct Debit

Please fill in the whole form using a ballpoint pen and send to The Bible Reading Fellowship, 15 The Chambers, Vineyard, Abingdon OX14 3FE.

Service User Number: | 5 | 5 | 8 | 2 | 2 | 9 |

Name and full postal address of your bank or building society

To: The Manager	Bank/Building Society
Address	
	Postcode

Name(s) of account holder(s)

Branch sort code

Bank/Building Society account number

Reference

Instruction to your Bank/Building Society

Please pay The Bible Reading Fellowship Direct Debits from the account detailed in this instruction, subject to the safeguards assured by the Direct Debit Guarantee.
I understand that this instruction may remain with The Bible Reading Fellowship and, if so, details will be passed electronically to my bank/building society.

Signature(s)	
Date	

Banks and Building Societies may not accept Direct Debit instructions for some types of account.

This page is intentionally left blank.